Cambridge, Massachusetts: Ghosts, Legends & Lore

E. Ashley Rooney

Schiffer Publishing Ltd
4880 Lower Valley Road Atglen, Pennsylvania 19310

Other Schiffer Books by E. Ashley Rooney

Berkshire Ghosts, Legends, & Lore, 978-0-7643-2797-1, $14.95

Lexington, Bedford, and Concord: Ghosts, Legends & Lore, 978-0-7643-3115-2, $14.99

Other Schiffer Books on Related Subjects

Ghosts of the Bridgewater Triangle, 978-0-7643-3006-3, $14.99

Boston's Haunted History: Exploring the Ghosts & Graves of Beantown, 978-0-7643-2874-9, $12.95

Haunted Massachusetts, 978-0-7643-2662-2, $12.95

Library of Congress Control Number: 2009922513

Designed by RoS
Type set in Abaddon/News Gothic BT

ISBN: 978-0-7643-3255-5
Printed in the United States of America

Schiffer Books are available at special discounts for bulk purchases for sales promotions or premiums. Special editions, including personalized covers, corporate imprints, and excerpts can be created in large quantities for special needs. For more information contact the publisher:

Published by Schiffer Publishing Ltd.
4880 Lower Valley Road
Atglen, PA 19310
Phone: (610) 593-1777; Fax: (610) 593-2002
E-mail: Info@schifferbooks.com

For the largest selection of fine reference books on this and related subjects, please visit our web site at:
www.schifferbooks.com
We are always looking for people to write books on new and related subjects. If you have an idea for a book please contact us at the above address.

This book may be purchased from the publisher.
Include $5.00 for shipping.
Please try your bookstore first.
You may write for a free catalog.

In Europe, Schiffer books are distributed by
Bushwood Books
6 Marksbury Ave.
Kew Gardens
Surrey TW9 4JF England
Phone: 44 (0) 20 8392 8585; Fax: 44 (0) 20 8392 9876
E-mail: info@bushwoodbooks.co.uk
Website: www.bushwoodbooks.co.uk

Photo Credits:
Red Heart on a Grid Background © Kirill Alperovich. Ghost sepia © Fiona Butler. *Photos courtesy of BigStockPhotos.com.*

Frontispiece.
Harvard and the City of Cambridge. *Courtesy of D. Peter Lund*

Acknowledgments

Many of us don't quite understand ghosts. In this book, I have told or retold these ghost stories from a fictional perspective, trying from my comfortable place in the twenty-first century to make sense of the past. Throughout the work, I have endeavored to be as true to historical fact as possible. The copy-editing of Barbara Purchia made this work that much easier. The photography of my husband, D. Peter Lund, and Siobhan Theriault certainly highlight this illustrious setting.

Contents

Introduction:

Welcome to Cambridge

Nicest place that ever was seen,
Colleges red and Common green
Sidewalks brownish with trees between.

-- Oliver Wendell Holmes

†††††††††

Cambridge, Massachusetts, is one of the most densely populated cities in the United States. Noted for its cultural diversity, its population ranges from recent immigrants to affluent professors, from street performers to descendents of the Puritans. Over 100,000 people live within this 6.5 square mile city that is world renown for the two prominent universities that call it home: Harvard University and the Massachusetts Institute of Technology (MIT). The former, which celebrated its 350th anniversary in 1986, is the oldest institution of higher learning in the United States. The latter is known for its dedication to advancing and educating students in science, technology, and other areas of scholarship.

Cambridge's charming "squares" offer many cultural activities, shopping, dining, and sightseeing.

† Harvard Square, which encompasses the brick walls of the nation's oldest university, offers cafes, bookstores, boutiques, and entertainment.

† Kendall Square, the home of MIT, is the base for many technology-oriented enterprises.

† Porter and Inman Squares have several restaurants as well as many diverse artistic and cultural attractions.

Host to many street fairs and festivals and home to many students, Cambridge is a fun city.

† June's Cambridge River Festival has music, art, food, and a variety of hands-on art-making activities for kids.

† In August, a Caribbean-style carnival features music, parades, dancing, and food, representing the diverse cultures of the Caribbean islands.

† Each September, Cambridge celebrates the Italian Festival of Healing Saints Cosmas and Damian.

† October's Head of the Charles Regatta is a two-day event, where sailing fans watch racers from all over the world compete along the Charles River.

Founded in 1630 as Newtowne, Cambridge was much bigger in area at that time than it is today. It was one of a number of towns (others were Boston, Charlestown, Watertown, and Roxbury) established by approximately seven hundred Puritan colonists of the Massachusetts Bay Colony under governor John Winthrop. An ardent Puritan, Winthrop believed fervently that the Anglican Church needed to be brought into a state of purity as it had been in the time of Christ. Convinced that God would punish England for its heresy, he, along with other Puritans, obtained a royal charter for the Massachusetts Bay Colony and pledged to establish a new colony in New England. Elected governor of Massachusetts by the company in London, Winthrop and his fellow Puritans arrived in Salem on June 22, 1630.

Unlike the Pilgrims who settled Plymouth, Massachusetts, in 1620, many of the Puritans had titles, property, and a college education; their leaders were well-trained scholars. Along with their money, furniture, and other worldly goods, they brought with them a vision of the future. As Winthrop stated, they wanted their new colony to be a biblical witness, a "city on a hill," or an example of biblical righteousness in church and state to be admired by the world.

The Puritans had originally intended that Newtowne would be their capital. The site was on a small hill overlooking the marshes on the north bank of the Charles River. It had an adequate fresh water supply, well graded land, and the potential for productive farming. At high tide, the Charles River was deep enough for vessels traveling the ocean and yet protected the city from assault. The Puritans laid out Cambridge as a fortified town and built a channel to accommodate vessels.

Puritans continued to immigrate to New England because of the weak English economy and the Crown's lack of tolerance for religious dissent. By the end of 1634, the town had about sixty families.

Unlike many New England towns, the streets were laid out in an orderly grid, bounded today by Eliot Square and Linden Street, and Massachusetts Avenue and the river. Each family owned a house lot in the village, planting fields outside the village, and a share in the common land. Cambridge Common is all that's left of the original cow common or grazing land, which lay within the angle between Massachusetts Avenue and Garden Street. Here, herdsman drove herds of goats, swine, and cattle to pasture every day. Later it was transferred to the town of Cambridge as a training ground. Soon, Newtowne had a meetinghouse on the southwest corner of what eventually became Mount Auburn Street, plus a school and a marketplace. The ferry was the only easy way to travel to Boston until the Great Bridge was built in 1660; the ferry landing, built in 1635, was at the end of Dunster Street.

By 1636, Cambridge paid the largest tax of any town in the colony, but its inhabitants needed to find more land to raise cattle, which was their main source of income. Consequently, the General Court gave them all of Arlington (known as Menotomy or West Cambridge) and most of Lexington (called Cambridge Farms). The townspeople found keeping cattle across the river to be inconvenient, however, and Lexington was too far for people who valued nearby neighbors and ready access to the meetinghouse.

The Puritans lived in a world where church and state were one. They believed that religion and education were essential elements of a Christian community. In autumn 1636, six years after the Puritans' arrival, the Great and General Court selected Newtowne over Salem as the location for the colony's first college. This was a fortuitous move for the village as the college promised much business for artisans and shopkeepers, a market for the farmers, and a cultivated society for the gentry.

In 1638, the city's name was changed to "Cambridge," since many of the leading colonists had graduated from Cambridge University, England. The colonists believed that the name "Cambridge" would reflect its status as the center for higher education in the colony.

Reverend Douglas Glover, a dissenting minister, never made it to the colony, but his printing press and printer did in 1638. They found a safe home in the house of President Dunster of Harvard College, who later made the widow Glover his wife. That printing press did all the printing in the British colonies in America until 1674 when Boston got a press. Thanks to Reverend Glover and the foresight of President Dunster, Cambridge and Harvard College were quickly established as the literary and philosophical center of the colonies. Today, the City of Cambridge is known throughout the world as one of the great and continuing intellectual centers.

By 1759, Cambridge had about 1,500 residents. The majority of the inhabitants were descendants of the original Puritans — farmers, artisans, and tradesmen — and some slaves. The meetinghouse and its minister, Dr. Nathaniel Appleton, dominated the life of the community. It established the morals, mores, and manners of the villagers. Almost everyone belonged — except for the Anglicans or members of the Church of England. They kept to themselves on Brattle Street or, as it was often called, Tory Row.

At the advent of the American Revolution, Cambridge was a quiet New England farming village. Its satellite communities such as Newton and Lexington were now separate towns; others, such as Arlington, had their own meetinghouses and schools. Its heart was the common and the college.

Harvard University's Johnston Gate bears two plaques telling the story of the founding, funding, and naming of Harvard College. *Courtesy of D. Peter Lund*

On the night of April 18, 1775, William Dawes rode out Massachusetts Avenue on his way to Concord to warn the colonists that British Regulars were on the march. The following afternoon, after the Battles at Lexington and Concord, several Cambridge Patriots died in a skirmish with retreating British Regulars at the corner of Massachusetts and Rindge Avenues. The provisional government confiscated many Loyalist estates, and their owners fled for their lives. The American Revolution had begun.

Within days, more than 20,000 armed New Englanders were camped in Cambridge under the command of Major General Artemas Ward. The militia took over the vacant Tory estates, the empty Christ Church, and Harvard's brick buildings for officers' quarters, barracks, and administrative buildings. Soldiers camped on the common, which also became the training ground. As more militia continued to arrive, tents, huts, and shanties sprung up all over town. Ultimately, temporary barracks were built for the colonial soldiers.

As memorialized in "Arsenal Square" and "Magazine Street," Cambridge established the first state arsenal and one of the principal powder magazines. By order of the Committee of Safety, Harvard College canceled classes on May 1. Students either donned uniforms or resumed classes in Concord that October. The night before the Battle at Bunker Hill in June 1775, approximately 1,200 American soldiers lined up at the edge of the common. The President of Harvard stood on the steps of a gambrel-roofed, elm-shaded house to pray for the soldiers as they stood solemnly before him. Students did not return to Cambridge until June 1776.

†††††††††††

On June 25, 1775, General George Washington departed Philadelphia for Massachusetts. On July 3, 1775, he halted his horse under an elm on the common in Cambridge, drew his sword, and formally took command of the Continental Army, a rag-tag group of farmers, artisans, and workmen, who were still rejoicing about their defense of Bunker Hill on June 17. His speech emphasized unity:

> *... it is to be hoped that all distinction of colonies will be laid aside, so that one and the same spirit may animate the whole, and the only contest be, who shall render, on this great and trying occasion, the most essential service to the common cause in which we are all engaged.*
>
> *-- George Washington*

Gen. Washington used the Vassall-Craigie-Longfellow House as his headquarters for nine months in 1775-1776. As the siege dragged on, he sent for his family. His wife Martha Washington and her son arrived in Cambridge December 11, 1775, and remained there until the army departed in April 1776.

In the fall of 1777, the English and German prisoners (or "Convention Troops") captured at the Battle of Saratoga were held in Cambridge until they were transported back to England. Neither the townspeople nor Harvard College wanted to house these prisoners. Ultimately, several hundred British and German officers, wearing their swords, lived in Cambridge as "paying guests." By the end of the war, the formerly pretty Cambridge showed the wear of a year's occupation by the militia and use as a prison camp.

Cambridge in the early nineteenth century was a country village surrounded by stonewalls, fields, and farms. The Charles River, with its miles of mudflats and salt marshes, separated it from Boston. Approximately twelve shops stood around the square, which was known as the marketplace up to the 1830s. Supposedly, a giant elm tree stood where the subway kiosk now stands.

Cambridge and its university attracted many scholars and their families, e.g., Edward Everett, George Ticknor, Margaret Fuller, John Quincy Adams, Louis Agassiz, and the Dana, Holmes, Longfellow, and Lowell families.

Between 1790 and 1840, Cambridge grew rapidly. Its population was approximately 6,000 with most of its new citizens coming from Boston or escaping from rural New England. Most of its population worked as artisans or small tradesmen or as laborers in livery stables or boardinghouses.

The construction of the West Boston Bridge (now Longfellow Bridge) in 1793, connecting Cambridge and Boston, drastically changed the economy. In 1809, when the Canal Bridge, adjacent to the present Museum of Science, was completed, East Cambridge was opened for development. Former estates and marshland became prime industrial and residential districts. The inexpensive land, water transportation, and proximity to Boston in such areas as Cambridgeport attracted furniture and glass factories. Soon after, turnpikes and roads were built, connecting different sections of Cambridge to the bridges. By the 1840s, railroads came into use, leading to the development of Porter Square.

When the potato blight struck Ireland in 1845, thousands of rural Irish, destitute and without resources, landed in Boston and Cambridge. Many lived in East Cambridge, laboring at unskilled jobs in the glass works and furniture factories. The close-knit Irish community centered on the Catholic Church. By 1855, twenty-two percent of the adults in East Cambridge were Irish-born.

Northwest Cambridge had abundant clay that had been used to make bricks since colonial times. Massive brickyards, drying kilns, and clay pits sprang up between Massachusetts Avenue and Alewife Brook. Housed in crowded workers' cottages, many Irish worked in the clay pits and brickyards, meeting the rapidly growing demand for manufactured products.

In 1846, Cambridge was incorporated, uniting three villages: Old Cambridge, Cambridgeport, and East Cambridge. Its commercial center also began to shift from Harvard Square to Central Square, which became the downtown of the city. On April 10, 1861, MIT was incorporated — two days before the Confederacy bombarded Ft. Sumter.

By the 1880s, Cambridge was a growing manufacturing city with horse-car transportation linking it to Boston. Pleasant residential neighborhoods spread out from Massachusetts Avenue. One country road led north to Porter's tavern — the birthplace of the Porterhouse steak — and where Porter Square is today. Later, stockyards and taverns flourished in this area. The descendants of the Puritans probably weren't very pleased with the rum selling and drinking, fast driving, and street racing on the Lord's Day.

Around the turn of the twentieth century, Italian, Polish, and Portuguese immigrants began to arrive, settling primarily in Cambridgeport and East Cambridge. French Canadians and Russian Jews also came at this time, settling in North Cambridge and Cambridgeport, respectively.

Today, Cambridge is home to a culturally diverse population of over 100,000 residents. College students from around the world attend Harvard, MIT, and other institutions in the city. Technology-based enterprises, such as electronics, software, and biotechnology research, have replaced the manufacturing industries of the nineteenth and early twentieth centuries.

Part One:

GHOSTS

Have you ever had the hair at the nape of your neck prickle uneasily when you heard the creak of a stair or felt a sudden chill in the room? All areas have ghosts. These ghostly tales endeavor to give these spirits a past, a present, and perhaps even a future.

Chapter One:

Best Friends

Each friend represents a world in us, a world possibly not born until they arrive, and it is only by this meeting that a new world is born.

-- Anais Nin

When I received the questionnaire that hot summer day asking for my housing preferences — window open, window shut, single, double or more, smokers or non-smokers, that sort of thing — I didn't really know what I wanted. As an only child, I always had my own room and never had to share with anyone.

It was six o'clock in the morning when I stepped out of the cab in Harvard Square after a long, anxious night that had begun somewhere in Idaho. The sun was rising over the city of Cambridge. To me, dazed from a night of traveling and no sleep, Cambridge was like a city from a dream. My dorm room, in the soft brick building, was white with big south-facing windows, scarred pine floors, and a ceiling slanted like my vision of a garret. It was a small cell that contained two beds, two chests, two desks, one bookcase, and two closets. My roommate's clothes were already spilling out of one closet. A soft-spoken blonde from Tennessee, she said, "Just call me Mary Sue." She wanted to major in economics. "I hear you meet really smart men in those classes." She licked her pouty lips slowly. "I'm not that smart book-wise, although I did well on all those tests to get in here. But I'm more interested in meeting people," she giggled, "if you know what I mean."

"Oh," I replied dully. Certainly, we weren't going to have much in common.

"What about you, Leslie?" she asked. "Don't you want to meet men here? Away from home? Without your parents hovering and worrying about your every move?" She rolled her big blue eyes and giggled happily.

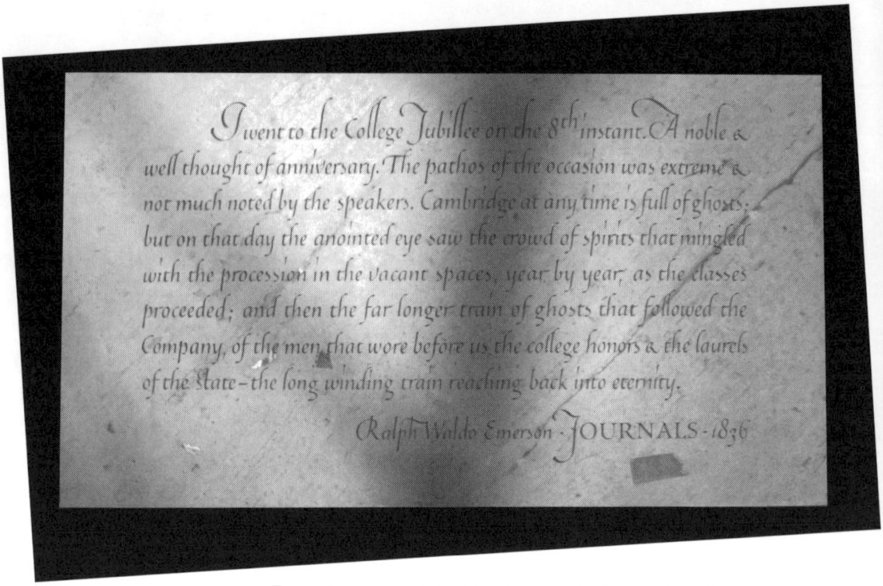

Even Emerson felt the ghosts at Harvard College. *Courtesy of D. Peter Lund*

Harvard Square. *Courtesy of Siobhan Theriault*

She must be an idiot, I thought. One of those girls who was only interested in men. "I guess," I replied slowly. I told myself that I had other more significant dreams. I wanted to make my mark on the world. A man would be good, but I didn't see that having a man would necessarily allow me to make that mark. So Mary Sue and I worked out an amiable arrangement. I studied, and she partied.

I was amazed at the beauty of New England in those first few weeks: the trees laden with apples, the clock towers and their pealing bells, the brilliant red leaves, and the groups of red-cheeked children playing soccer on the velvety field. I made no real friends and spent most of my time studying. Midterms came, and Mary Sue got As to my B+ in English Composition, Comparative Literature, and Analytical Geometry. She could party and still excel. I just plodded along. No parties, but many late nights! Usually, I could find something that made me feel good when I compared myself to another, but that didn't appear to be true in this case. She appeared to have everything.

On the other hand, I found that I rather liked Mary Sue in an odd way. She amused me. With her, I always had that sense that something exciting was about to happen. With circles of red high on her cheeks and disarrayed hair, she would come bouncing into the room, "Guess who I met?" Then she would tell me about the newest celebrity on campus, or how she had tried some weird new food like escargots, or stood up and sang "Dixie" at the local bar. Life took on a glow when she was around. I was the type of person who got up at the same time every morning, brushed my teeth in the same way, ate the same breakfast, and followed the same routine every day. I did my laundry on Wednesday nights and called my parents on Sunday. A major change for me was to go to Elsie's and eat their chicken salad sandwich for dinner rather than going to the dormitory's cafeteria. Now, sometimes Mary Sue got up; sometimes she didn't; sometimes she never went to bed! In addition to excitement, she added beauty to my plain humdrum life. With her, our room was no longer a monastic cell but a large airy room with a breeze fluttering in the white curtains. In the corner, near her desk, she had added a small round table with a teapot and fresh flowers — always. She picked them up in the Square: roses, chrysanthemums, and carnations.

Mary Sue liked to vary her pattern, to live life with Auntie Mame-like flourishes. She made me laugh, even though I knew she was breaking the rules that I believed in. I washed my underwear by hand as my mother had told me; she just threw hers into the washing machine and later admired the new holes. While I dutifully read *Crime and Punishment* for Modern European Lit, she read the "Cliffnotes" while reclining on some grassy hillside batting her eyelashes at a good-looking guy. I would fuss about the upcoming exam and point out how she hadn't studied, and she would reply: "Honey, I'm OK. And you're studying enough for both of us." And she did well.

You might ask what I got out of this relationship. Do you remember Cinderella and the wand-swinging fairy godmother? That's who Mary Sue was. She helped me change my hairstyle from a ratty half-ponytail/half bun to a soft wavy curl. She threw away my cheese and crackers, chocolate chip cookies, and hot cocoa mix and substituted low fat popcorn and instant coffee. I began to lose weight. My complexion cleared. I wasn't beautiful, but I looked much better. As I lost weight, she made me toss my baggy t-shirts and sweats and took me shopping for classy jeans.

When she was around, we would go for walks on those chilly November afternoons when the sky was like lead and the clouds were racing by. She would talk to all the passers-by and pat their dogs, exclaiming, "He's so gorgeous," in this loud insincere voice or what I thought was insincere. But the dog owners didn't seem to think so. They smiled and talked about their wonderful animals and how much they loved them. Meanwhile, I would stare at the sidewalk and wonder why I couldn't be like that. She brought fun into my life. She made me see the beauty of the small Oriental rug that she put between our beds, the single rose in the vase, and the tiny jewel-like painting she hung on the wall.

I wasn't quite sure what she got from a relationship with me, but I knew that she had no women friends. She didn't have anyone with whom she could chat about menstrual cramps, clothes, or soap operas. We shared laughs, a few sweaters, shopping at the Coop, and occasional meals at the Wursthaus. She talked and talked—and I...listened.

The other women stayed away from her. On the other hand, the men certainly didn't. Many men knew my name because Mary Sue was my roommate. They thought she was the most wonderful person in the world. If she didn't return their phone calls, they would ask for me, hoping that I would tell them where she was.

Someone in our dormitory posted a hooking up chart on the cinder-block wall just inside the laundry room. Down one side of the chart someone wrote our names and then assigned us letter grades:

V for Virgin,

J for Jobs,

H for High Flyer,

B for Boring.

I had been assigned a "B," and Mary Sue was an "H" with *Easy* scribbled next to it.

I didn't like being considered "Boring," but I figured that it was better than what I could have been called. It was easier for me to concentrate on my studies than to go to Passim's or Bartley's Burger Cottage and appear to be casually interested in the Harvard students. By not going, I didn't have to know whether they were interested in me or not.

Mary Sue partied hard. Often she brought home men she had met at bars. She would be giggling so hard that she was almost unintelligible. I would sigh, pick up my books, and leave. Before the Thanksgiving break, I realized that I had spent many weekend nights on the floor of our hall studying while she "entertained" a young man in our room. I gave her a wastebasket—to have as her own—and left out brochures about Genital Warts and HIV. Looking back, I was earnestly and tensely playing the role of responsible big sister. I had nightmares about the dangerous men that she could meet on the dark Cambridge streets. She would hug me hard, "Leslie, I love that you care about me. I'll be all right. Don't you fret now."

No matter how hard I studied, she always had better grades than I did. In the classes we had together, she was number one; I was number two. Her paper on Henry James was an A+; mine just an A. In Music Appreciation, she wrote a paper about how awful "Boris

Godunov" was, having only listened to the first act. I sat through all of "Salome." She got the A; I got the B+.

Once I went with her to a bar, where the music was insanely loud and beer formed puddles on the floor. The smoke hovered near the ceiling; people danced and talked over the music. Mary Sue was dancing with anyone who would ask her. Men who wanted her attention would talk to me, telling me their sad stories, hoping that she would smile upon them. Someday they may think of me, the plain roommate who sat beside them at the bar.

The phone was always for her, and it was always some man who would hope that she was available for breakfast, lunch, or even dinner. "Please," they would plead. "Have her call me?" She would tear up my carefully written notes, laughing. I felt sorry for the men. They were nothing but tickets to adventure for her.

You might wonder why I didn't just find another place to live. Often, I asked myself that, but Mary Sue was everything I wasn't. I was the moth flying around her light, waiting for the next bit of excitement. She was beautiful, long-limbed, flirtatious, and one of those people for whom everything came easily. As different as we were, I learned from her. I was no longer the size of a small truck — not even a compact car. When I stressed out, I went for a walk and found that I was walking further and further. Occasionally, the two of us would go out for a walk. Despite our differences, we had a good time together, but I wondered what my life would be like without her? Not as much fun, but I wouldn't feel this envy.

One night in late January, when the cold winds blew off the Charles and the snow clung to our feet, Mary Sue didn't return. Usually, she always appeared by midnight, so I figured she would show up. She would come striding down the dormitory hall, laughing, hugging those she met, and calling everyone "honey." But she didn't come. I walked outside and looked up at the sky encrusted with stars. All I could hear was the hiss of the powdery snow and the crunch of my feet. By noon, I went to the Dean, who must have gone to the police, because they appeared at suppertime, asking questions about Mary Sue and whom she hung around with. Had she run away? No, I didn't think so. Suicide? No, she certainly had not committed suicide. She was happy. Life was good for her.

I responded to them to the best of my knowledge, but still no Mary Sue. When I went to bed that night, I dreamed about her. She wasn't smiling or laughing this time. She looked pale, washed out, and was wringing her hands. I heard a door opening, and then shutting. I yanked the comforter over my head. Mary Sue was just fine. She was off with some hot guy.

But she didn't appear — except in the headlines. She had vanished — except in my dreams. I would see her striding into our room, carrying a bouquet of red carnations, tossing her hair, and calling out, "Leslie! Guess what?" But those were just dreams. At the end of January, her parents came and took her clothes and stuff. They left the little round table and the vase with its now very dead Christmas carnations. I bought Twinkies and Snicker bars and twisted a rubber band around my hair. My life had come to a halt in shades of grey as if I were frozen in place.

The dirty snow melted in patches, and then new snow came in the beginning of February. Dagger-like icicles cracked and plunged from the roof. In the dorm, people wore wool socks and drank hot cider. They played bridge and talked about what they would do when they graduated. I went to my classes and straight back to my room, bypassing all these chummy souls. No one mentioned Mary Sue nor did I. Now that she was gone, I was first in my classes.

Most people went home for spring vacation; I stayed in Cambridge to work on my paper on William Blake and his *Songs of Innocence*. The writing wasn't going well. Everything I read had just a little Mary Sue in it; a tint, a touch, and an inflection. She didn't take over, but she was never absent. Her little table stood in the corner with its vase of shriveled carnations.

In the third week of April, the weather turned suddenly unseasonably warm. The sun shone on the muddy ground, the sky was blue, and the trees displayed bright green froth. William Blake and his Songs really bored me. Late one night I went for a walk — one thing I hadn't foregone after Mary Sue disappeared. I was behind in school; there were papers to write and exams were looming, but the trees were in chartreuse bud and the air was heavy with spring sounds and smells. A shadow fell on my face. A hand reached for mine. "Leslie, you need to find me. You can't just let me disappear." I felt a cold chill run through me. I told myself that I was just stressed out. I walked until the sun disappeared, and a cool damp wind blew my hair. There was a party in a building across the way. Laughter and Foreigner's "Juke Box Hero" floated through the night air. I pushed away my memory of Mary Sue's face. I tried to think about what I would do this summer. Go home or stay here in Cambridge? Would I even come back next year? Would I ask for a new roommate? So many unanswered questions, I told myself. When I heard a giggle in the distance, I ran inside to my room and hid under my covers.

I woke the next day to a chilled sunlight and the thump of Judas Priest down the hall. I stared myopically at my room. It seemed different. The dust motes danced about Mary Sue's little table. Budding daffodils stood in the vase. I went back to sleep.

That afternoon I walked all the way to Fresh Pond. Daylight was waning as I approached a circle of dancers, swirling and twirling at the far side of the pond. The setting sun seemed to explode in my face like a firework. I shielded my eyes with my hands. It was the same familiar landscape, yet it had transformed into something different. The music ebbed and rose, ebbed and rose. The dancers made a wide circle and began to move; swaying and humming, bending and clapping. I was in a vast spinning universe. I felt so connected — I had never felt that way. The wind carried their hair streaming out behind them. I thought about joining in, which made me chuckle. I certainly had changed if I was thinking about doing something like that.

The setting sun reddened the water as they danced with abandon. Mary Sue would have been right in the middle of all those dancers, I thought. She would have been waving her hands, kicking up her long legs, and laughing. I focused on the wavering flames of the fire. Suddenly, one of the couples broke from the group and started turning and whirling. Others followed, flinging their arms out, uttering shrill cries. The area was fraught with passion. A breath of wind lifted the leaves of the surrounding trees. The luminous sunlight became insubstantial, and something appeared to be moving within the shadows.

Down the path, through the creaking ancient trees, came a long-limbed blond. Mary Sue stood over me. "Hey there, honey. I missed you." She reached out a hand. "Come walk with me and tell me how you are."

We walked and talked as only two women friends can. The sun was low, burning gold through the trees, casting our long distorted shadows on the ground before us. Branches swayed and creaked, and invisible night creatures began to stir in the dark. Then, the moon came up, and everything became silent and strange. There was no wind, not a bird sang, not a leaf stirred. There was no sound but the crunch of our shoes on the gravel path and the whistle of the wind in the trees. We continued walking, talking quietly. As the birds began to rustle and the grey chilly dawn appeared out of the midnight blackness, we reached an empty lot. Mary Sue said, "I have to go."

"No," I said.

"I can't cross over until you find my body."

"No, no, no! You can't leave again."

"It's time for me to leave, and you need to bury me."

I buried my face in my hands.

Grimfaced, Mary Sue pulled me. "Come." She began walking.

"In there? That empty lot? With all that garbage?"

"Yes." I reluctantly followed her through the overgrown grass, stepping over the rusty metal, the old rags, and plastic bags. We walked in between the junked cars, the abandoned tires, and a derelict refrigerator. The grass brushed my legs. It was still and silent in the frosty dawn. I wished a bird would sing, but not even a crow called. My head hurt, and there was something not quite real about any of this — something like a dream.

"This is where I live now," Mary Sue said. "Look!" She pointed at a large piece of cloth imprinted with what appeared to be red flowers wrapped around something long. Blonde hair protruded from one end. The lighting was changing, the breeze blew back my hair, and there was a shimmering of something withdrawing. The air was cold — like an early morning mist. Something was snapping at my heels, gaining speed in the shadows, getting ready to leap.

I gasped and turned away, moaning.

"Don't you dare turn away, Leslie. I cannot sleep until my body is found."

I began to pull away. "No, no," I cried. "No," I screamed and began to run across the frosty grass. The sun was looming over the horizon by the time I arrived back at the dormitory.

Red and white tulips stood in the vase.

2

Chapter Two:

The Bishop's Palace

A lovely eighteenth century wooden mansion is hidden away among the buildings of Harvard University. Today, it's the oldest part of Adams House. General Johnny Burgoyne was held prisoner there after his surrender at the Battle of Saratoga in 1777 during the American Revolution. People say that he haunts it, but you have to wonder why General Johnny returns there...where he was unhappy and cold. My supposition is that the shuffling steps heard and the figure seen is that of East Apthorp, the builder of the mansion. He had everything: brains, position, and family, but he pushed his fellow citizens too far and they pushed back. So East occasionally visits his lovely mansion.

††††††††††

Intelligent and friendly, East Apthorp had a distinguished background. The son of Charles and Grizzell Eastwicke Thorpe, he was raised as the son of a wealthy British man. A prosperous merchant, his father was the paymaster and commissary of the British forces quartered in Boston. East went first to Boston Latin School, America's first public school, and then to England, where he entered Jesus College, Cambridge, earning a Bachelor of Arts in 1755 and then a Master of Arts in 1758. He won the Chancellor's Prize for eminence in classical learning and the Members' Latin Dissertation Prizes. Elected a Fellow of his college, he was ordained an Episcopal priest.

His friends marveled. "My father says East is so intelligent," raved one young lady dressed in flowered silk. "He says Apthorp is a classical scholar and a cleric. His family is well respected."

"And he has such sensitive feelings," added her friend. "I just wish that he would look at me with more adoration."

"There is someone in the colonies, I hear."

"Well, maybe he won't go back. Who would want to live there?"

"I hear it is a dreary place. Cold too," she shivered.

But East did return to Massachusetts Bay Colony in 1759. He came home with a taste for well-made, beautifully designed things. Yes, the impeccably tailored and groomed East Apthorp was an up and coming young man.

Most Cambridge residents were descendants from the original Puritans and lived near the Common and Harvard College. A small group of very aristocratic Royalists lived on "The Road to Watertown" (today's Brattle Street), known as Tory Row. Set far back from the street, their spacious clapboard houses had lovely rooms, where their owners entertained royal representatives and toasted his Majesty. Uninvolved in the life of Cambridge, the Royalists made their livings from inherited wealth, West Indies plantations, and trade. Their possessions were many, their wealth large, and they were Anglicans, of course! Unlike the more serious-minded Puritans, they knew how to have a good time. They lived in prosperity and happiness, enjoying music, dance, and snuff. Puritans certainly did not approve of such habits.

The Royalists began to build an Anglican church. They already had engaged their charming young rector, Dr. East Apthorp. They arranged to pay Mr. Apthorp twenty pounds sterling and provide him with a parsonage. What an opportunity for young East! In turn, he contributed his salary to the building fund. Perhaps he could give such a generous gift since he was marrying the daughter of a judge.

The Cambridge gentlemen selected as architect Peter Harrison, then of Newport, Rhode Island, who had designed Boston's King's Chapel ten years earlier. He designed for Cambridge what has been called one of the best-constructed churches in New England. It still stands in the middle of Harvard Square.

Back in the 1760s, Cambridge was a very small town. There were fruit trees and garden plots, pigpens and sheep commons, a brewery, and a row of outhouses. The college was clustered near the Square: it included Harvard, Stoughton, and Massachusetts Halls, Holden Chapel, and the President's House, now known as Wadsworth House. The college staff included the president, two professors, four tutors, and a librarian; there were 180 students.

Today, the Bishop's Palace is a lovely Colonial house with an old-fashioned garden. *Courtesy of Siobhan Theriault*

As Christ Church was being built, East Apthorp began building himself a stately Georgian mansion at #10 Linden Street across from the church. In August 1761, he married Elizabeth, the daughter of Judge Foster Hutchinson of the Superior Court of the colony of Massachusetts and the granddaughter of Governor William Shirley. Yes, East was well on his way to greatness. "After all," he said to Elizabeth, "as the rector of the Anglican Church in Cambridge, I need a suitable mansion."

She nodded happily, "And I, my dear, need an appropriate house suitable for entertaining others and our English visitors. And hopefully we will be having a larger family soon ourselves." She patted her stomach gently.

"That would be wonderful, my dear." East kissed her heartily. "I do want a son and heir."

"And I a lovely home," she smiled up at him.

The Cambridge Congregationalists, however, not expecting that a member of the clergy would require such an extravagant house, were outraged. "That is unseemly," sniffed one matron to her husband.

"Now, dear, it's just a house."

"No, it's a palace. Look at those columns!" she replied. "I hear it has hand-printed wallpaper too."

"Well, my dear, he was educated in England and probably would like to walk in their Anglican footsteps," replied her husband.

East, on the other hand, believed in thinking big. As far as he was concerned, the size of his success would be determined by the size of his beliefs. He had to think big to be big, he told himself. If people didn't understand that, well, then they didn't understand anything. Apthorp House would show the world of Cambridge who he was.

In 1760, the cornerstone of the church was laid, and Sir Francis Bernard, the recently appointed governor of the Massachusetts Bay colony, was present. On October 15, 1761, the church, with its rows of high square box pews and wineglass pulpit, held its first service. The ardent Reverend East Apthorp preached a sermon entitled "On the Constitution of a Christian Church" to the gentlemen in their cocked hats, laced coats, and white silk stockings. Many non-Anglicans attended out of curiosity about the Anglican Church, an organization that had brought into their community the same elements of popery and confusion that had driven their forefathers to leave England.

When the service was over and East had duly shaken everyone's hand and promised to print his discourse, he walked out of the church, across the Cambridge Common, to Apthorp House, which stood with admirable proportions, its Ionic pilasters rising high, on the crest of the long ridge that mirrored the meandering path of the Charles River. One of the largest and most magnificent houses in Cambridge, it had a projecting central pediment, columns, and well carved ornamental details. Grounds that originally extended toward the Charles River surrounded it.

Although East Apthorp was known as a very amiable young man with engaging manners, his house was more than his fellow citizens could bear.

One morning after meeting, one somberly garbed Puritan said to several others, "The Church of England has been wanting to establish a bishopric here for a long time. I don't like what I see before me."

"I hear they have installed a mighty fine organ in the church," added another. "I expect they want everyone to tithe and to genuflect too."

"They certainly aren't living humbly with God."

"I say," interrupted a third, "that mansion is like the palace of one of the more humble successors of the Apostles."

John Adams wrote, "A great house, at that time thought to be a splendid palace, was built by Mr. Apthorp at Cambridge."

Even today, it's known as the Bishop's Palace, although it's now a Harvard college dormitory.

Yes, our imprudent young minister had built a wonderfully grand home with a broad entrance hall, which originally extended through the house. The well-proportioned staircase with its spiral twisted balusters reached a spacious landing at the middle of the house. The high-ceilinged reception room had carved wainscots, panels, and moldings and hand-printed wallpaper. The fireplace was lined with blue delft tiles with Scripture allegories. Its rooms were filled with Chippendale mahogany furniture.

The people of Cambridge were not fond of the Anglicans. Attendance remained small. Moreover, the people of Cambridge did not like that the Church was built directly in front of Harvard College and that the rector's house resembled a bishop's palace.

His fellow citizens were quite jealous. "That house is built in quite a grand manner. It is typical of the wealthy Anglicans to have built such a grandiose structure. They flaunt their wealth, you know."

"He's much too young for that type of house," sniffed one matron.

"I don't now about his youth, but he certainly is inexperienced. Doesn't he know how angry people will be?" asked her friend.

"He has gone and established himself an Episcopal See, I tell you."

East's beautiful home served to escalate the distrust with which Puritans viewed the Anglicans. Although the Puritans had left England to pursue religious freedom, they were loath to offer the same freedom to others. They did not easily tolerate dissent. Seeing the richness of the house, the citizens of Cambridge believed that Dr. Apthorp aspired to become a bishop and to bring back the Church of England to their fair little village.

Thus it came to pass that Dr. Apthorp, in his desire to add still another noble specimen of Georgian architecture to the buildings of Cambridge, made many people quite unhappy with his opulent mansion. When he published his views in a pamphlet entitled "Considerations on the Institution and Conduct of the Society for the Propagation of the Gospel," he had a war upon his hands. The pastor of Boston's West Church, Dr. Jonathan Mayhew, and he fought a pamphlet war. The resulting controversy, in which Apthorp House was dubbed "the Bishop's Palace," forced Dr. Apthorp and his family to leave his beautiful house in 1765 and return to England, where bishops were respected rather than ridiculed. There, he was awarded titles and positions and lived ever after. After his death, some believe, he returned to his beautiful home in Cambridge, where he has been seen ascending or descending the well-proportioned staircase. It's only in death that he can enjoy it.

The Revolutionary Years

Another Tory, John Borland, bought the house and added a third story, but he too was forced to leave Apthorp House when his royalist sentiments became unpopular at the start of the American Revolution in 1775. The house then served both as headquarters and barracks for General Putnam and his Connecticut troops until about the time of the Battle of Bunker Hill. When the siege of Boston ended in March 1776, Putnam was ordered to New York, and the house was, in all likelihood, vacant for a time.

In October 1777, the General Court of Massachusetts was officially informed that General John Burgoyne had allowed his dwindling army to be surrounded by the Americans and had surrendered at Saratoga. According to the terms of the surrender, Burgoyne, with more than 5,000 soldiers in his command, was to be quartered in Cambridge until they were transported back to

England. Abigail Adams wrote to her husband in 1777, "Burgoyne is expected in by the middle of the week." The Committee of Safety leased Apthorp House to Burgoyne. The "Bishop's Palace" was now the jail for an English general.

The winter of 1777-78 was an uncomfortable one for the British prisoners. The barracks built for the besiegers of Boston were now occupied by her vanquished foes, but they had no wood to burn and the winter was cold. Like many subsequent tenants in Cambridge, Burgoyne complained bitterly about the lack of furnishings and the exorbitant rent he was forced to pay. Legend has it that Burgoyne's ghost still haunts the house.

The Nineteenth and Twentieth Centuries

After the Revolution and throughout the nineteenth century, the Apthorp House passed quietly through a succession of owners until it was incorporated into Harvard's Gold Coast of private dormitories in the early 1900s. When any student was perceived as living too high and mighty, he was told that Dr. East Apthorp would come to visit him and set him straight!

Today, Apthorp House is the master's residence for Adams House, a dormitory on Bow Street. Under Harvard's house system, groups of students spend their last three years in the same residence hall, each of which has a corresponding master's house. The staff is available for counseling, tutoring, conversation, and, on many Friday afternoons throughout the school year, tea. There is talk of a ghost in the house — as delicacies for the afternoon tea disappear suddenly — but nothing is said definitively.

3

Chapter Three:

The Haunted Church

For almost 250 years, Christ Church, a parish of the Episcopal Diocese of Massachusetts and a National Historic Landmark, has occupied Zero Garden Street in Harvard Square. The second oldest church in Cambridge, the building retains much of its original shape and structure. Many famous people have worshipped within its walls; armies and vandals have destroyed parts of it; and a *ghost* dating from the early days of the American Revolution resides there.

††††††††††

Around this time, five or six wealthy Cambridge Royalists petitioned the Society for the Propagation of the Gospel in Foreign Parts to build an Anglican Church in Cambridge, where it could serve surrounding towns and those Harvard College students who had been raised in the Church of England. The Society focused on providing the ministry of the Church of England to colonists. Puritan colonists who looked upon the Church of England with suspicion, however, had settled the Massachusetts Bay Colony. In one of those ironic twists of fortune, they had disagreed with the Crown's lack of tolerance for religious dissent, but the Puritans were just as intolerant. Unlike the Pilgrims, they were religious bigots.

Christ Church is one of the more famous pre-revolutionary buildings in the United States. Peter Harrison, who some call America's "first architect," designed this historic church. A self-taught architect, he was inspired by the English architects who were building grand Baroque buildings. His design allowed the church to be taken apart and enlarged as the congregation outgrew the space. Christ Church's interior today still resembles the 1759 original, except that the "box" pews no longer remain.

The wood frame church rests on a granite foundation built from stones that served as ballast on incoming ships to Boston Harbor. *Courtesy of A. P. Richmond*

The wealthy Anglicans did not spare any expense in furnishing their church. A fine organ made in London, a bell weighing over 1,500 pounds, a silver christening basin from Reverend Apthorp's mother, a folio Bible from Mrs. Faneuil, and two folio prayer books from Mrs. Lechmere were the chief gifts. Initially, Anglican families rented the box pews, with the money being used to pay the rector. In 1778, vandals broke the organ and scattered its pipes. The bell was recast in 1831 and again recast in 1859. Near the door were two small pews for the wardens, whose wands of office stood in the corners, and these pews still remain.

Most of the founding members of Christ Church lived nearby, on Tory Row. In 1759, at the age of 26, East Apthorp (see "The Bishop's Palace") became the first rector of the church, whose mission was "to minister to English families in Cambridge and students of Harvard." At the opening service in 1761, a prayer for George III was said.

After Dr. Apthorp left, Reverend Winwood Serjeant arrived in Cambridge in June 1767 and took charge of the church. During this time, Governor Hutchinson presented the church with the William and Mary communion service that was still in use in 1903. In a letter dated March 12, 1774, Mr. Serjeant writes:

> *The populace is almost daily engaged in riots and tumults... They made a second destruction of thirty chests of tea. Political commotions run extremely high in Boston.*

Three months later, he wrote:

> *Boston is in a terrible situation and will be much more so if they do not submit to government before fall; the town will be absolutely ruined.*

Already Major John Vassal, John Borland, East Apthorp, and other Tory aristocrats had abandoned their homes in early summer and sought protection of the King's forces in Boston. Thomas Oliver remained till September and left his home, known as Elmwood, only when an armed mob appeared in front of the house and demanded his resignation from the Mandamus Council created by Parliament. He, too, sought the protection of General Gage. The only member of Christ Church left in Cambridge was the mild-mannered Judge Lee.

Revolutionary Times

At the beginning of the American Revolution, Cambridge was a quiet New England farming village.

During the first months of his stay in Cambridge, Gen. Washington worshipped in the meetinghouse with Dr. Appleton. When Martha Washington arrived in Cambridge in the middle of December, she insisted on an Anglican service at Christ Church. At the expense of Judge Lee, hasty repairs were made, and the Washingtons are said to have sat opposite the third pillar from the entrance door when they attended a New Year's Eve service in 1775. Of course, the good Puritans were flabbergasted. Royalists worshipped at Anglican services — not Americans!

Colonel Palfrey, the acting clergyman at that New Year's service, read the sermon and instead of praying for the king, which is incorporated in all Church of England services, prayed that King George III might be enlightened. He asked God to:

> *Be with thy servant the commander in chief of the American forces...strengthen him that he may vanquish and overcome all his enemies...and grant that we may in due time be restored to the enjoyment of those inestimable blessings we have been deprived of by the devices of cruel and bloodthirsty men...*

But the Revolution rolled on, and the church was closed until 1790.

The Ghost

Later, the church building was reopened for the internment of the English and German prisoners (or "Convention Troops") captured at the Battle of Saratoga in 1777. Neither the townspeople nor Harvard College wanted to house these prisoners. Ultimately, several hundred British and German officers, wearing their swords, lived in Cambridge as "paying guests." By the end of the war, Cambridge showed the wear of a year's occupation by the militia and use as a prison camp.

One day in June 1778, an English prisoner, Lieutenant Richard Brown of the twenty-first Regiment, was riding down Prospect Hill, Somerville, and lost control of his horses. When a sentry challenged him to halt and show his pass, Brown, who was trying to control his horses, merely pointed to his sword, which he retained by terms of the surrender as one of Burgoyne's officers, to indicate his rank and privilege. At this point, the young sentry ran up to the carriage and shot Brown through the head. Brown's funeral on June 19, 1778, was the only service held in Christ Church where English, German, and American officers and soldiers prayed to God together. Brown was entombed with military honors, and his coffin added to the other caskets in the vault beneath the church in the Vassal tomb.

Supposedly it was during the Revolutionary War that the church was plundered, ransacked, and defaced. All through the 1780s, the church remained desolate and neglected, but by 1790, Reverend Dr. Parker of Trinity, Boston, reopened it.

Over the years, many Harvard students, from Richard Henry Dana (author of *Two Years Before the Mast)* to Teddy Roosevelt (who was asked not to continue as a Sunday school teacher because he would not become an Episcopalian), attended Christ Church during their college years. In 1968, Martin Luther King and Dr. Benjamin Spock held a press conference in the Parish Hall, where they first proclaimed their opposition to the Vietnam War and formally joined the anti-war movement of the time.

Today, the church, which was declared a National Historic Landmark in 1960, is an oasis of peace. In the still air you can sense a presence, however. The ghost of British Lieutenant Richard Brown is thought to still walk about the sanctuary. Visitors may see that the candles are suddenly extinguished and hear odd shuffling noises and doors bang — yet no one is there. Is it our young British lieutenant who never made it back to England?

4

Chapter Four:

Hide and Seek

When we were young, we used to visit friends and play Monster while the adults sipped their frosty cold martinis, ate sticky orange cheese spread on crackers, and politely conversed about the state of the world and the neighbors. Monster went like this: one person would hide. Once he or she had counted to fifty, the other players would try to find the monster without letting anyone else know. So as the seeker you had to be very quiet. When you opened the door to that closet or looked under the bed and saw the monster, you crawled in beside him. Ultimately, everyone but the remaining seeker would have crawled in with the monster while the last seeker ran frantically around the house, with only his footsteps echoing up and down the stairways. Often the last person would announce loudly to the silent house, "I give up. You win." Then we would all come chortling out and make great fun of him. Sometimes the game took a different turn, and no one could find the monster in the eaves, closets, alcoves, under the beds, or behind the large chests. The monster would squirm into his hiding spot, waiting for the footsteps to come close, but no one would come. Then whoever played the monster would come out, arms outstretched rather like Frankenstein, and we all would run away, screaming.

Such games aren't unique to us. During the nineteenth century, groups of young people would hold sing-alongs and put on brief theatrical performances in dazzling costumes. Sometimes, they would play childhood games such as Sardines or Hide and Seek. Often they sat around the fireplace and told stories. This is one of my favorites....

††††††††††

Christmas was coming, and the house was decorated with pine garlands, holly, and greens. A large ball of mistletoe hung in the hall. The Christmas tree, which stood on a side table, was decorated with candy-filled paper cornucopias, cleverly folded doilies, colorful bits of ribbon, and beeswax tapers placed in specially designed tin candleholders. Gaily wrapped presents were under the tree. This fanciful vision of delight lightened the winter gloom in the mahogany-paneled hall.

Edward Wentworth, the elderly host, bid the maid, "Now keep the folding doors to the dining room closed until dinner is ready."

"Yes, sir."

"Of course, everyone knows it, but tonight's the formal announcement of Marie's engagement to Lovell."

"He's a fine man, sir. You will like having him as a member of your family."

"Absolutely. He's already been a good man to work with in the firm. Now, you remembered the champagne glasses?"

"Yes, sir."

"So when dinner is ready, open the doors and lead everyone to the dining room. I will take my sister in, my aunt and uncle can follow, and then the eight young people."

His guests were amazed when they saw the large, brilliantly lit room with its pyramid of lights sparkling from the dark pine boughs decorating the fireplace. Victorian trumpet vases stacked on silver candy compotes were centerpieces on mirrored plateaus. They reflected the light from the candles. The buffet was filled with sweets and savories, including a fruit and nut topiary, a date pyramid, and a bowl of candied grapefruit.

Dressed in holiday finery, family and friends feasted upon a Christmas Eve dinner of raw oysters, bouillon, potatoes, peas, roast beef, and flaming figgy pudding with brandied hard sauce. They toasted the health of Marie and Lovell with the champagne. One young man marveled at the refinement of the particular bottle served. Another said, "I would call it more delicate than refined."

"Hush!" said Marie. "It tastes like the stars of the evening."

"Nicely put, my dear," said her fond papa.

The eight young people debated about whether they should play charades, but then the ancient aunt, dressed in purple satin and bedecked with diamonds, announced, "I will play the piano." She sat down and began to play a waltz. Feet began to tap, and sleepy eyes sparkled. The host asked his sister to dance. Two of the young men rolled back the big Oriental rug so everyone could dance on the polished oak floor. The fire crackled and snapped, and the host beamed with pride. His only child, Marie, would be Lovell's bride, making the friendship between the two men even closer. They would live in this house, run his business, and life would be good.

"Play a polka," urged one young man.

"Oh, why not try the new two-step," said another.

"Only if you have the music," retorted the pianist. "How about a reel instead? Those I know by heart."

Each gentleman began to chassez out with the lady on his right hand. Marie whirled around the floor in her brilliant red velvet dress, laughing. At the end of the dance, she exclaimed, "This is wonderful fun, but my new shoes are pinching my toes. Let's do something else."

"Like what?" asked her fiancé, fingering his mustache.

"Let's be children again, Lovell, and play hide and seek."

"Oh my. At my age?"

"You're not an old fuddy-duddy yet!" She laughed. "Come. Before we become staid married folk, we should play one last time."

Lovell frowned. "Please, dear," Marie entreated.

"If you wish, my sweet. Give me a kiss."

"I'll give you a kiss when you find me," she laughed. "You are the seeker. Now count to 100." And off she and the other young people ran. Her father sat and smiled, wishing his wife was still alive to enjoy these lively young people.

After Lovell counted to one hundred, he went looking. He found young Sophie, pretty Blanche, Jane, Thomas, Richard, and Ben, but he couldn't find Marie. "Where are you," he called. There was no response. He thought he heard a thump, but no one else did, even when he hushed everyone. They called and called. Then, with much laughter and "do you remembers," they all went looking, but no one found Marie in her pretty red velvet dress. They cried, "Come out, come out wherever you are." But Marie didn't turn up. They checked the third floor eaves, the storage space off of the front stairwell, and the passageway between the two largest bedrooms. All seven young people went floor to floor, room to room, closet to closet looking for her, but she was not to be found. Sophie, Blanche, and Jane began to look perturbed, but Richard laughed at their sad faces. "She's just hiding on us. It's a big joke."

"That sounds like her," exclaimed Ben. "Remember when we played before, and she hid on top of the attic rafter."

"That's where she is now," shouted Lovell. And off he went.

He came back ten minutes later looking dismayed. "No luck, I'm afraid."

Marie's father laughed. "She really outsmarted you this time, Lovell. She's going to run you quite a race once you're married."

"Well, I'll have to put a stop to that," retorted Lovell.

Blanche yawned. "It's almost 2 a.m. Why don't we call it quits? She'll show up in the morning."

"You think?" asked Jane.

So they each thanked their host, reassured Lovell that Marie would reappear, laughing at how well she had tricked them, and went home.

Marie didn't appear the next morning. Neither Lovell nor her father went to church services; instead, they searched each room, one by one, hoping to find bright-eyed Marie in her red velvet dress rubbing the sleep out of her eyes. The Christmas presents sat under the beautifully decorated tree, but no one even approached them. Their focus was on finding Marie's hiding spot — *and Marie* — not on Christmas gifts. The two men looked for her under the beds, in the dank cobwebbed cellar, up the chimneys, the closet nooks, the attic, in the old oven...but they didn't find her.

Days, weeks, and years went by. Marie had disappeared. Her heartbroken father died, leaving the house and his business to Lovell.

††††††††††

Lovell moved into the large rambling house. All the floors and stairways were carpeted so heavily that he couldn't even hear the servants at work. Yet, occasionally, he heard footsteps overhead, but when he'd go to check, he was the only person in that part of the house.

At night he would hear footsteps, but no one was there...

Pale-faced, stammering servants left his employ, saying that the house frightened them. They too heard the footsteps at night; sometimes, they said, they felt a presence in their rooms as if someone was standing over them.

Lovell discussed the odd experiences with a friend.

"Often when I'm reading, I hear someone running — quickly, lightly — along the hall on the floor above us. There never is anyone there for I have often run up the stairs to see, but the upper story of the house is dark and empty."

"Maybe they are hiding in a closet," suggested his friend.

"I checked very carefully to be sure nobody is hidden away. All is empty and still."

"Is that all?" asked his friend.

"Occasionally, there is a cold draft yet no windows or doors are open."

"Any other signs of a ghost?"

"Yes, there are these dark, shadowy movements, and if I look up quickly enough I see a human shape wafting out of the room to disappear."

"Maybe it was a natural shadow or your imagination."

"Or maybe it's a ghost." Lovell looked down at this hands dotted with liver spots. "Sometimes, as I walk along the hall, I feel as if someone is following me, reaching out to touch me."

"Why do you stay?"

"I'm not sure. I think the house is trying to tell me something."

††††††††††

As Lovell aged, he became more of a hermit. Slowly, he sold off the furniture in the upper floors and closed off the rooms. The curtains faded; shingles fell off; paint peeled; the porch stairs rotted. The house looked like an old derelict. When Lovell appeared in society, people whispered, *"He is the man whose bride disappeared,"* or they would point at him and mutter, *"He never married. He still looks for his bride."*

One Christmas Eve, Lovell dreamed about an old oak chest in his attic. All night in his dream, he prowled about it, trying to open it, but he couldn't find the latch. Yet, when he pulled on the lid, it remained shut. He was sweaty and tired when he woke, rubbing the sleep out of his eyes. Wearing his old tatttered dressing robe, he climbed the winding stairs to the attic. There, behind a large walnut armoire, he found an oak blanket chest festooned with cobwebs. He wasn't sure whether his heart was thumping or the chest was knocking when he raised the lid and found a skeleton clad in a brilliant red velvet dress. When asked about it later, Lovell told people that her lips formed a kiss.

But he no longer heard the sound of someone running through the house. No one reached out to touch him in the shadowy hall, and Lovell soon realized without his ghost he was quite lonely indeed.

5

Chapter Five:

Dreams of Glory

Whenever he went down town,
We people on the pavement looked at him:
He was a gentleman from sole to crown,
Clean favored, and imperially slim.

And he was always quietly arrayed,
And he was always human when he talked;
But still he fluttered pulses when he said,
"Good-morning," and he glittered when he walked.

And he was rich - yes, richer than a king -
And admirably schooled in every grace;
In fine we thought that he was everything
To make us wish that we were in his place.

-- Edwin Arlington Robinson

††††††††††

Andrew Craigie was an ambitious man. He had always wanted to live in a big house on an important street. Once he saw the Vassall house on "The Road to Watertown" (today's Brattle Street; aka Tory Row), he knew he had to live in it one day. The house was one of seven manor houses surrounded by fine gardens and outbuildings and set far back from the street.

In 1759, John Vassall, a wealthy royalist, built the handsome house. There the Vassals entertained royal representatives, toasting his Majesty in fine wines, and wined and dined the local Royalists who lived in the other six houses. The occupants were generally related to one another and made their living from inherited wealth, West Indies plantations, and trade. In 1774, when the Revolutionary fervor and the people of Cambridge became too much of a presence in their lives, the Vassal family hastily abandoned the house and fled to British protection in Boston.

Today, the Vassall-Craigie-Longfellow House is usually referred to as the Longfellow House. The U.S. National Parks Service administers this National Historic Park site. *Courtesy of Siobhan Theriault*

In June 1775, General George Washington, Commander-in-Chief of the newly formed Continental Army, used the house as his headquarters and home while he planned the Siege of Boston. John and Abigail Adams, Benedict Arnold, Henry Knox, and Nathaniel Greene visited Washington there. Martha Washington joined her husband in December 1775, and the two stayed in the house until March 1776. Having housed the Commander-in-Chief of the Continental Army and the nation's first president, the mansion had an illustrious history. In 1791, Andrew Craigie bought the mansion.

Andrew, a Boston apothecary, was a go-getter. The Massachusetts Committee of Safety appointed him commissary of medical stores on April 30, 1775. His job was "to take care of the medical supplies and to deliver them out as ordered by this committee" (Worthen, *Andrew Craigie*). He treated and cared for the wounded at the Battle of Bunker Hill in a makeshift station behind the battle lines. On July 4, 1775, he was appointed medical commissary and apothecary of the Massachusetts Army. When Congress reorganized the Army's Medical Department in 1777, Andrew was appointed the first American Apothecary General. His duties included procurement, storage, manufacture, and distribution of the Army's drug supplies. An enterprising Yankee, Andrew also developed an early wholesaling and manufacturing business. He knew how to generate wealth.

By the end of the war, Andrew was a wealthy man involved in land and money speculation. He participated in the failed (and questionable) Scioto Affair, purchasing five million acres in Ohio and planning to sell them to French immigrants. That didn't prevent him from purchasing the Vassal-Washington house. He added a rear ell, expanded the library into a 20- by 30-foot ballroom with its own entrance, and built a greenhouse (which created great criticism) and an icehouse. Andrew had china designed, furniture built, carpets woven, paintings bought, and wines laid down. He entertained the celebrities of the day, including Talleyrand and Prince Edward, the father of Queen Victoria. He had so many guests that he had to order more of his privately designed china. Life was good for Andrew. All he needed was a wife.

In 1793, the thirty-nine-year-old Andrew met twenty-two-year-old Elizabeth, the daughter of a widowed Nantucket clergyman. Elizabeth acted as her father's hostess, housecleaner, and cook. She didn't have much time to meet eligible men. Just two months before meeting Andrew, she had met a man while walking the Nantucket beach one foggy morning. The next day she met him again. By the third day she experienced a rush of excitement as she saw him walking towards her. His blue eyes twinkling, he strode through the sand. When he reached her, he touched her cheekbones lightly as if he were wiping away a speck of dirt. Her throat hurt. She wished the two of them could stay frozen in this moment. He let his fingertips move across her mouth for a long second.

Later, he told her that as the youngest son, there was no inheritance waiting for him. He would have to make his own fortune. A shrewd New Englander, Elizabeth knew that marrying a poor man meant hard work. *His caresses are light as whispers, but even they aren't worth living a life of drudgery*, she said to herself. *I cannot live like this for the rest of my life.* She smiled through her tears as she gazed into his loving eyes. Crestfallen, he begged her to wait for him while he went west to seek his fortune.

††††††††††

Two months later, she visited friends in Beverly, Massachusetts. One day Andrew Craigie appeared in an impressive coach. After he had paid her some significant attention, Elizabeth commented, "He appears to be very wealthy."

"He is. I hear he has a beautiful house too," commented her friend.

"Hmm." To the daughter of a widowed Nantucket clergyman, wealth in hand was very tempting. Her beloved was still searching for his. He might never return, and she was already 22 years of age, which was getting rather old for a bride in those days.

"Marrying him would mean all sorts of wonderful things for you, Elizabeth," added her friend. "You wouldn't have to work so hard. You would have servants! You could get what you wanted."

"Maybe," Elizabeth looked thoughtful. "Does he know many important people too?"

"Of course. Under George Washington, he was in charge of medical services at Bunker Hill, Cambridge, Germantown, and Valley Forge."

But Andrew wasn't the only person who was ambitious...

Elizabeth wanted off that elbow of sand on the Atlantic Ocean. She wanted to get away from those long cold winters when the wind howled, the surf pounded, and the desolate moors were open to the endless sky. No longer did she want to wash her father's underwear, make his supper, and look pious during his sermons. She sealed her lover's letters away in a small camphor chest and hid it in her closet. That was her past; her future was going to be glorious.

Compared to Nantucket, Cambridge was a metropolis. It had twelve shops in its square. Although most of its residents worked as artisans, small tradesmen, or laborers, many scholars and their families were attracted to Cambridge because of Harvard University. Elizabeth could escape the drudgery and the boredom of her island life by marrying Andrew.

††††††††††

Elizabeth enjoyed her move to Cambridge and the lovely home, which ultimately would mean so much to the American people. She followed Andrew from room to room, touching the handsome furniture, stroking the colorful rugs, and fondling the sparkling crystal. She gloried in the subtle colors and the rich textures of the wallpaper, the richness of the oil paintings—and, most important to her, the scent of money. Andrew had transformed the property into a 140-acre estate in the middle of Cambridge. He had added a number of outbuildings, side porches, and an ell onto the back of the house.

The months went on, and the couple's differences became obvious. Elizabeth liked to read; Andrew liked to acquire properties and things. She liked to speak French; he liked to wheel and deal. He talked about banks and land; she liked discussing Voltaire's *Candide* and his trials and tribulations. She felt no passionate thrills; he saw no admiring smiles. Their meals became silent, their conversations infrequent. They had no children.

One day she received a letter from her lover:

> Dear Elizabeth,
>
> Rejoice. I am coming home to you. My great uncle has left me his estate of over 100 acres north of Boston. I will speak to your father, and we will marry. Love.

It's too late, she thought. I'm already a married woman. In those days, the daughter of a clergyman didn't abandon a marriage, even if the marriage had no heart. Sadly, she folded up her lover's letter and hid it with his others.

On foggy days, she would see her blue-eyed lover standing in her closet, saying, "You should have waited for me." When he stepped out of the shadows, he moved toward her and put his arms around her. She could feel the frissons of delight crawl up her spine. A look from him, the press of his hand on her flesh, his lip against her ear... overwhelmed her. When he held her close in his arms, she could swear she smelled smoke and could hear a distant rumble. Instead, she would close the door firmly and go downstairs to direct the servants, admire her beautiful china, practice her French, and wait for another day to end.

By the mid-1790s, Andrew had spent a great deal of money on his house and been involved in several risky real estate investments. Then his New York business agents, Horace and Seth Johnson, went bankrupt. Convinced of the economic opportunity in Boston, Andrew purchased the marshlands, grazing fields, and a few farms near Lechmere Point. In conjunction with a Boston businessman, Harrison Gray Otis, Andrew formed the Lechmere Point Corporation and built the Canal Bridge (ultimately known as Craigie's Bridge) across the Charles River. By 1811, the Corporation laid out a street grid that extended into the surrounding marshlands and donated the land for a new county courthouse in East Cambridge and $24,000 for the building's construction. They retained renowned Boston architect Charles Bulfinch to design the building, which still stands today on Cambridge Street. In 1813, they sold their first parcels of land for industrial purposes.

Land sales were slow, however, and Andrew's debts mounted. His creditors began to harass him. "Where's our money?" they would question. "You owe us." If he went outside his house, they accosted him. They talked to the neighbors. Poor Andrew became a recluse; shut away in his beautiful mansion, he avoided creditors and ventured forth only on Sundays, when his creditors left him alone. Sunday was a holy day, after all. Hiding in his palatial house, he became a pale wrinkled echo of himself as he reluctantly sold off his possessions to pay his debts. Ultimately, he lost everything but his home (now known as the Vassall-Craigie-Longfellow House). In 1819, Andrew Craigie, who had such dreams of grandeur, died forgotten...the architect of his own misfortune.

Elizabeth, who had married Andrew for his wealth, fired most of the servants. She wished she could shut off all the rooms, except for the few that she still used. She didn't want to dwell on the past. It was best to leave the past alone, undisturbed, sealed up—never to be opened again. But she couldn't afford to do that. She needed to survive. Grudgingly, she leased the greater part of her house to polite young Harvard students. Three future Harvard presidents, Jared Sparks, Edward Everett, and Joseph Emerson Worcester, plus numerous professors, including the widowed Longfellow, lived there.

Dressed in black, she lived in the back rooms reading Voltaire. She rarely opened her closet anymore. Her lover's letters remained in the camphor chest in the recesses of the closet, gradually disintegrating and crumbling into dust, as did her beauty. Occasionally, passersby would see her face, pale and watchful as a ghost's in the light of her lamp, but then gradually it would slide back into the dark. Her life went forward, but she had come to a halt in the deep recesses of her house as if she were living in a snapshot, frozen in place.

††††††††††

After her death, Nathan Appleton purchased the house and gave it to Longfellow and his daughter Frances as a wedding gift in 1843. In 1959, the Association of Military Surgeons of the United States established the Andrew Craigie Award, which is given annually to a pharmacist in recognition of career accomplishments in service of the advancement of the pharmacy within the federal government (Worthen, *Andrew Craigie*).

6

Chapter Six:

The Hovering Ghost

I heard the bells on Christmas Day
Their old familiar carols play,
And wild and sweet
The words repeat
Of peace on earth, good will to men!
-- Henry Wadsworth Longfellow

††††††††††

I realized several months ago that I believed in ghosts. I've never seen one, but I know my father talked to my mother as if she was still there and, of course, she wasn't. She was long dead, but he shared everything with her and he would tell us how proud she would be of us. It was as if she were right in the room — just seen through a glass darkly, like the Bible says. Of course, a lot of people think you're nuts if you believe in ghosts. But I suspect they are thinking of those white-sheeted ghosts like in Dickens' *Ghost of Christmas Past*. I think ghosts are with us all the time — we *can't* see them, but we *can* sense their presence.

Let me start at the beginning...

Sometimes it's really hard to have a perfect parent, who is the idol of so many people: queens, presidents, and other famous people. It's even more difficult to have a parent who is one of the best-loved poets and who *talks to* ghosts. That's what my Father does.

My Father, Henry Wadsworth Longfellow, was born February 27, 1807, in the bustling seaport of Portland, Maine. He told me that when he was a little boy he had an infected foot, and there was talk that he might lose it. Luckily, he didn't, but, as a result, he didn't do as much racing and running around as his brothers and sisters. Instead, he immersed himself in books and reading. He found he particularly liked poetry and that he could rhyme words and make jingles. Soon he was writing poems, although his Father demanded that he become a lawyer. By the time he was a student at Bowdoin College, magazines in Philadelphia and Boston were publishing his poems. Still his father insisted that, "Nobody earns a living at writing poetry." When Henry asserted that he could, his father said to him, "We're not wealthy people, Henry. It is impossible to earn a living in the United States as a writer."

I expect that Father said to himself, "I'll show him." That's what I would have done. When he graduated from college, Father went to Europe. He had letters of introduction to famous men, but he preferred to talk to the farmers, the tradesmen, and the innkeepers. He traveled far, learning languages and meeting other writers such as his idol, Washington Irving. When his sister died, he came home. He was 22 years of age and started teaching Spanish and French at Bowdoin. In his time there, he wrote textbooks in French, Italian, and Spanish because none were available and a travel book, *Outre-Mer: A Pilgrimage Beyond the Sea*.

In 1831, he married Mary Potter, who encouraged him to keep writing his travel sketches, although he had major teaching duties. In December 1834, Father received a letter from Josiah Quincy III, president of Harvard College, offering him the Smith Professorship of Modern Languages position; however, the offer stipulated that he spend a year or so abroad. Father happily accepted, and he and Mary went abroad, where she died in Rotterdam, the Netherlands.

Grief-stricken, Father wandered about Germany and Switzerland until he met the Appleton family of fashionable Beacon Hill, Boston, who were also traveling in Europe. Seventeen-year-old Fanny Appleton took charge of him. She took him for carriage drives and long walks. They went on boat trips; they talked and talked. Father began to feel much happier. When he returned to Cambridge and the new professorship, he knew that he would see Fanny again because she lived in Boston.

He rented a room at the beautiful old Craigie House on Brattle Street. He had visited the house before and was smitten by the view of the gleaming Charles River at the foot of the lawn. Just a short walk from Harvard, it had once been the home of George Washington. Mrs. Craigie was a widow and definitely strange, he told me. She spent her days reading in a back room and looking down upon the young men to whom she rented rooms. Father taught, read his favorite German and Italian poets, wrote poetry, and often walked across the Cambridge Bridge to Boston to see Fanny. (Eventually, this bridge, which is also known as the Salt and Pepper Shaker Bridge, became known as the Longfellow Bridge.)

Everyone liked the handsome young writer with his long flowing hair and flowered waistcoats. He was publishing his poems more frequently and becoming a well-recognized poet. Father made many friends. Some of them, like Nathaniel Hawthorne and Ralph Waldo Emerson, were also important writers.

By this time, Father was trying to persuade Mother to marry him. However, he had made a serious mistake; he wrote *Hyperion*, a novel that told the story of his pursuit of her. She was not pleased and broke off their relationship. Father kept writing and teaching; people praised his poetry, but he missed Fanny. He wrote about the plight of slavery in this country and the need for all to pursue happiness. He wrote about the spreading chestnut tree and the village smithy and the wreck of the Hesperus. Finally, Fanny and he met again. Seven years after he came to Cambridge, in July 1843, they married. Mrs. Craigie had died, and my grandfather, Nathan Appleton, bought them the Craigie House as a wedding gift.

Soon Father and Mother filled that big beautiful house with friends and family. There were five of us: two boys and the three girls whom Father described in "The Children's Hour" as "grave Alice and laughing Allegra and Edith with golden hair." I'm the one with golden hair.

My parents were rarely separated. My well-educated Mother happily shared Father's pursuits. They would spend hours discussing poems and stories. I could almost see them glowing when they looked at each other. Once, while reluctantly attending a ball without Mother, Father lamented that without her "the light seemed dimmer, the music softer, the flowers fewer, and the women less fair."

Life was good. Father wrote poems that were easy to understand and their verses were easily memorized; they expressed a joy, a spirit of optimism, and faith in life. Mother supported him and loved us all. Many friends came to visit. One night Nathaniel Hawthorne asked him if he had heard the story of how the Acadian farmers were banished from their village. After hearing the story, Father wrote one of his most favorite poems, "Evangeline," describing the betrothal of an Acadian girl and the deportation of the Acadians from Nova Scotia. The poem was so popular that father began to consider retiring from Harvard so he could write more. He had hoped to become a great American writer, and his dream was becoming a reality. In 1854, he resigned and devoted himself to his writing. In June of that year, he began *The Song of Hiawatha*:

By the shores of Gitche Gumee,
By the shining Big-Sea-Water,
Stood the wigwam of Nokomis.

Never had a poem been so successful. Sculptors made statues of Hiawatha and artists painted pictures of him and Minnehaha. The book was translated into other languages, and everyone all over the world became interested in American Indians. Then Father decided to tell the story about one of our ancestors on his mother's side: John Alden and Priscilla Mullen. He wrote "The Courtship of Miles Standish," where Priscilla asks, "Why don't you speak for yourself, John?"

By then, Boston and Cambridge were the focus of what has been called the "flowering of New England." Oliver Wendell Holmes called it the "the hub of the solar system." Here in New England began all those new "isms": abolitionism, feminism, Transcendentalism, and Unitarianism. And my father was right in the middle of it.

Everyone loved my Father and his poems. He wrote another novel and more narrative poems on topics of national interest. One of his most beloved poems is about the bravery of a man riding into the Massachusetts night to warn his fellow American colonists that British soldiers were on the march:

Listen my children and you shall hear
Of the midnight ride of Paul Revere,
On the eighteenth of April, in Seventy-five;
Hardly a man is now alive
Who remembers that famous day and year.

People sent him stacks of letters and surprising gifts. One gave him a fragment of the casket holding Dante's remains; another enclosed carefully mounted, exquisite specimens of seaweed because he wrote the poem "Seaweed." Father would open letters

The block-long Longfellow Park culminates in the Longfellow Memorial, sculpted by Daniel Chester French in 1913. It features Longfellow and low relief sculptures of characters from six of Longfellow's epic poems. *Courtesy of D. Peter Lund*

LONGFELLOW
1807-1882

from his admirers at breakfast, and we would all listen spellbound as he read them aloud. Mother would nod her head in agreement when the writer praised Father.

When Abraham Lincoln was elected President in 1860, Father was so happy. At home, we forgot the war talk and played happily. Father wrote:

> *I hear in the chamber above me,*
> *The patter of little feet*
> *The sound of a door that is opened*
> *And voices soft and sweet*

During those years, we were embraced in love. Our parents told us stories, we played, and we had wonderful visitors. But then Mother died — suddenly and violently — and all the joy was gone.

I was only seven when Mother died. My oldest brother was fourteen; and the youngest, five. I still remember my tears. It was so hot that July. Mother even put my hair in a net to get it off my neck. That day, she had trimmed some of my curls to preserve in sealing wax. While we were at the park, she melted a bar of sealing wax with a candle. Some burning wax fell upon her green muslin dress, one of her favorite dresses, and suddenly the breeze, which we had been waiting for on that sultry July day, gusted through the window, turning Mother into a flaming torch. She ran to Father's study in the next room, where he threw a rug around her to extinguish the flames. When he couldn't stop the fire with the rug, he tried to smother the flames by throwing his arms around Mother — severely burning his face, arms, and hands. The next morning she died; three days later she was buried in the Mount Auburn cemetery while the five of us cried.

Too ill from his burns and grief, Father did not attend her funeral. A week later, he became fully conscious and realized that his beloved wife was gone. His face was horribly scarred, and he had to stay in bed for another three weeks. Father grew a beard after his burns healed because he could no longer shave. We visited his room each day. We told him how much we missed him, but he was so sad. Everywhere he walked in the house, he told me later, he saw Mother: *She was in the library knitting, in his study talking and laughing with him, in the parlor dancing with us*. I think that ultimately he believed that she was there and because he believed *we* believed. Her spirit hovered over us all.

The first Christmas after Mother's death, Father wrote, "How inexpressibly sad are all holidays." A year later, he wrote, "'A merry Christmas' say the children, but that is no more for me." In Christmas 1863, we learned that my brother Charlie was severely wounded in the Tennessee campaign. In 1864, Father composed a poem, called "Christmas Bells," which became the Christmas carol "I Heard the Bells on Christmas Day." General Lee hadn't surrendered to Grant at Appomattox Courthouse yet, but Father's poem ended with the hope of peace on earth and goodwill to men. He was still grieving, but he held onto his optimism, his faith in others, and his belief that Mother was still there watching over us. Perhaps that is what we all want. Life has its good and its bad, but we can hope for peace and goodwill to others. And perhaps we could believe that Mother was still there — just not in human form. Father continued to write his poems, but most of his creative energy went into translating Dante's *Divine Comedy* published in 1867.

The following years were filled with honors. He was given honorary degrees at the great universities of Oxford and Cambridge, invited to Windsor by Queen Victoria, and visited the Prince of Wales. The Russian Academy of Sciences and the Spanish Academy asked him to be a member. Throughout all the honors, the ups and downs of life, he talked about Mother a lot — about all the good things she had done; her smile, her humor, and her great love for her family. So all those years, Mother was there — at least in spirit.

In his *Hyperion*, which Mother didn't like, Father said:

> *Look not mournfully into the Past. It comes not back again. Wisely improve the Present. It is thine. Go forth to meet the shadowy Future, without fear, and with a manly heart.*
>
> *Hyperion*, Bk. IV, Ch. 8 (1839)

I think that's what Father did, but he could do it because he believed that Mother was still there for him. And just maybe she was.

Part Two:

Legends

Legends are stories that have been passed down through the generations. Often, they are presented as history, but that may not be necessarily true.

Chapter Seven:

The Collector

He strolled about...recognizing from shelf to shelf every dear old book that he had had to put off or never returned to; every distinct voice of another time that in the hubbub of the world he had had to take for unlost or unheard.

Henry James, "The Great Good Place"

††††††††††

I'm told that one of the most prized bibliographical treasures in the world is a Gutenberg Bible. The first edition is four times as rare as a first folio of Shakespeare. I bought one for my oldest grandson, Harry, you know, because I couldn't go on that damn trip with him. The damp English weather plays havoc with my rheumatism, and I just couldn't take all that walking that one does when going to London. I'm getting old, and I pay for my excesses arthritically. Damn nuisance! My hands may be swollen around the joints and bent at the knuckles, however, but my mind is still sharp as a whip. Of course, it would have been fun to be there with Harry, although I must admit I was really looking forward to giving him that Gutenberg Bible. He would have been so pleased!

My name is Peter A. Brown Widener. I'm a capitalist, an Episcopalian, and a Republican, of course. I cast my first vote for General John C. Fremont in 1856. My daughter-in-law, Nellie calls me an old curmudgeon, although she smiles when she says it. It's good to see her smile these days because she has gone through a lot, you know. We both have. There are some people who insist that every time one door closes, another door opens but that's isn't always true. There are doors in life that are meant to stay closed, ones that lead to rooms filled with monsters, rooms crammed with grief, rooms stuffed with despair.

I'm a self-made man; I have an ancestor who was a captain on Washington's staff, but I was apprenticed as a — butcher's boy. I've come a long way from those two-meal days, although a while back when some friends and I were looking for food in a small city in the Mid West, I proved that I still could perform miracles when it came to trimming chops. I worked in the butcher shop long enough to learn the meat packing business; then, I opened my own meat stall: Peter A. B. Widener, Butcher. That turned into a string of meat stalls. Soon I was a political leader and organized the All Night Poker Players, a group of Philadelphia politicians. Oh, we had fun in those days!

My business really expanded when I got those Civil War contracts to supply mutton to the Union Army. Yes, indeed! I got ahead in the meat business because I was honest, and so the Republicans appointed me, the son of a poor German bricklayer, to the City Treasurership. Suddenly, I was on the way up.

I took my profits and, with my friend Bill Elkins, invested in Philadelphia's horse cars. The city was getting much too big for men to walk to work much longer. We first modernized them through a cable system like San Francisco had, but then I found that electricity worked better here in Philadelphia. I've been in the street railway business for upwards of forty years now. They call me the Richelieu of America's street railway system. My father probably didn't even know who Richelieu was! Horse cars began it all. Here I am, the son of a poor German bricklayer, a former butcher, and the newspapers call me a mogul! That's the United States of America for you. You can make a life for yourself here. From the Philadelphia Traction Company and all those trolley lines, I became the tramway magnate and went on to invest in Standard Oil, U.S. Steel, and the American Tobacco Company.

Life was good except when my wife died. I couldn't replace her; so I began investing in art and giving more of my time to my family.

When I came home from a trip to Europe where I bought all these paintings, I realized there was no room in my house. So I decided that I would build a new home for my family. My two sons, their wives, my four grandchildren, and I would all live together. The home would also house all my paintings, tapestries, and other fine things that I had collected in my annual trips abroad.

In 1907, I asked Horace Trumbauer to design my family a Georgian style mansion in Philadelphia. He outdid himself with a marble mansion that had one hundred and ten rooms. That's a lot of rooms for a man who used to sell beef! That's the American dream for you. Anyway, we called it Lynnewood Hall and filled it with European masterpieces and decorative arts. We had Van Dycks, an exquisite Botticelli, a splendid Titian, Corots, El Grecos, Gainsboroughs, Rembrandts, works by Turner, Constable, that new French man Renoir, and a Manet. I can't remember them all. You forget things at my age.

Funny, we can be surrounded by beauty, but that doesn't make the loss any better. The ghosts are still there. I expect sometime my son Joseph will donate many of the sculptures, paintings, and porcelains to the National Gallery of Art. That's where they belong.

Lynnewood is a great place. It includes a ballroom, swimming pool, wine cellars, a farm — even an electrical power plant. Nellie would say that I'm rambling now, but old men are allowed to ramble. Nellie was the wife of my son, George, who had taken over the running of the Philadelphia Traction Company and oversaw the development of cable and electric streetcar operations. He was a good sort. When he and Nellie, the daughter of my friend Elkins, married, they lived with me at Lynnewood Hall. All in the family, I say. I got to spend a lot of time with my oldest grandson, Harry, that way.

Harry once described our family as collectors. I collect paintings, his mother collects silver and porcelains, my son Joe collects decorative arts, and Harry collects books. He attended the DeLancey School in Philadelphia and the Hill School in Pottstown, Pennsylvania, where he first began collecting books. He loved Robert Louis Stevenson, but what boy doesn't? All that derring do and wicked pirates to boot. He once told me that he never traveled without a copy of *Treasure Island* and that he knew it by heart. Certainly, he told me about that one-legged seaman with a parrot on his shoulder many times. Harry's bedroom was stuffed with books piled on bookcases, tables, and chairs. But his room is empty now.

At Harvard, he studied history and became involved in the Hasty Pudding Club. During one school holiday, he told me that he was researching costumes for their theatrical productions when he became fascinated by George Cruikshank's and Thomas Rowlandson's portrayals of English life. In 1905, he purchased a presentation copy of Charles Dickens's *Oliver Twist* (London: Chapman and Hall, 1841), illustrated by Cruikshank—which he bought for $200. Harry told me later, "No matter how important a book or manuscript may be, I only want those which interest me." He collected books, I believe, because he loved literature. I never had the time to pay much attention to literature. I was always busy making money or so he tells me in my dreams.

It was the year 1905 that he met the Philadelphia collector and bookseller, Dr. A. S. W. Rosenbach, who some call the "Napoleon of Books" and the "Terror of the Auction Room." Rosenbach promotes the idea of collecting books as a means of investment. Bit different than U.S. Steel, but you get something of beauty to hold. The two quickly became close friends, browsing bookshops together. Nellie, who probably doted on Harry too much, spent $20,000 on color-plate books for him on his nineteenth birthday. That's something for the grandson of a butcher, don't you think?

Rosenbach was a persuasive man. He convinced Nellie that if Harry was to be a serious collector, he should own a set of William Shakespeare's four folios. Of course, Rosenbach had several in stock, so Nellie bought the second, third, and fourth folios for $8,700.

In September 1906, as Harry was beginning his senior year at Harvard, he bought the folio works of Ben Jonson, Francis Beaumont and John Fletcher, and Samuel Johnson's Bible. Its original owner had used it so much, Harry told me later, that several pages were worn out, and Johnson had copied them over in his own writing. That's something special, we agreed. Soon afterward Nellie bought him a presentation copy of Dickens's *David Copperfield.* That Christmas she gave him Dickens's agreement with his publishers for *Sketches by Boz*, some Rowlandson drawings, and a few other items. In March 1907, Nellie bought Shakespeare's first folio at a Sotheby's auction for £3,600, the highest price the folio had brought. Harry was developing quite a collection. When he visits me late at night, he tells me that he would have given old J. P. Morgan and his collection a run for his money.

Harvard's Libraries

For a young man, Harry was quite thoughtful. He knew that as a son of a wealthy man he should be generous with his estate. We often talked about what he would give to Harvard, which is an odd conversation to have with a man in his twenties. I wonder if he had a premonition.

Thanks to old John Harvard, the college had books — even before it had a building to contain them. Many others had followed his lead. John Hancock of Boston gave funds to purchase books, while political leaders such as John Quincy Adams, gave French and then Russian books. The college was strong in Hebrew and other Biblical books. It had Greek and Latin classics, Transactions of the Royal Society, the French Academy of Sciences and other scientific works, and a collection of the most approved medical authorities of the time. Within one hundred years, the university library became the largest in America. That fascinated Harry.

He told me that the Great Fire of January 1764 destroyed all the books, except for about four hundred, which were checked out at that time. Only one book donated by John Harvard survived the massive fire, which consumed the rest of the library. A student had taken the book in question out earlier that night. Realizing its worth, the student promptly took the book to the President of the College who, according to Harry, thanked him profusely, accepted the book, and expelled him for removing the book without permission! Tough old bird.

Harry decided that his collection of rare books should be given to Harvard University. He wanted it to be known as the "Harry Elkins Widener Collection."

Harry's Legacy

In the spring of 1912, Harry was 27. We had discussed taking a trip to England. As I said, I wanted to go, but it was too much for me. So Harry went alone and later joined his parents after he finished his whirlwind buying of books. They were due home April 17. My son George, Nellie, and Harry boarded the *Titanic* at Cherbourg, France. I knew many people of the people who embarked on that fateful voyage. I heard later that Benjamin Guggenheim and his valet returned to their cabins and changed into evening wear. Ben said, "We're dressed up in our best and are prepared to go down like gentlemen." *("Mr. Benjamin Guggenheim." Encyclopedia Titanica)*.

On that awful night, George and Nellie threw a private party in honor of Captain Smith in the *a la carte* restaurant. Later, Harry helped his mother into Lifeboat 4. Then he joined George and stood back. Supposedly, his friend Billy advised him to try for a boat, but Harry said, "I'll think I'll stick to the big ship, Billy, and take a chance."

When the *Titanic* sank April 14, 1912 — I'll never forget that date — more than 1,500 passengers and crewmembers died in the 31°F ocean. Harry, my son George, and their valet went down with the ship some four hundred miles off the coast of Newfoundland. Their bodies, if recovered, were never identified. Many just drifted away. We held a the funeral at St. Paul's Episcopal Church in Elkins Park and dedicated stained glass windows to their memory. But it wasn't really a funeral; there were no bodies; my son George and Harry were just absent — not dead. Somewhere Harry is still marveling at all those beautiful illustrations in *Treasure Island.*

The steamship *Carpathia* rescued Nellie and her maid. She says that Harry helped her into Lifeboat 4 and then helped other women. Some say Harry was about to step into a lifeboat that would have saved his life when he ran back to his cabin to retrieve a rare 1598 edition of Bacon's *Essais,* which he had purchased in London. But who could possibly remember in all the confusion that must have ensued? I just hope he went quickly, pondering the next book that he would like to own.

A broad flight of granite steps across the main facade of Widener Library leads to the door, which is behind a long colonnade of stone pillars. According to legend, the Widener donation specified that the library exterior was never to be altered, or else ownership of the building reverts to the city of Cambridge. As a result of this, Harvard has been creative in its renovation—even building a causeway to another nearby library through a large window. *Courtesy of Siobhan Theriault*

Nellie doesn't say much. She talks about how cold the night was and hearing the cries for help as one interminable wail gradually dying away. Then she said there was just silence except for the sounds of the lifeboats. The sound of that silence must have been awful.

Harry left his entire estate, valued at $150,000, to his mother. Because his father, his executor, also died, Nellie, the sole beneficiary, was made administrator.

Soon after her return home, Nellie wrote Harvard President Lowell notifying him of the terms of Harry's will and of her wish to build a small memorial library at Harvard to house her son's books. After Lowell and the head of the library visited her here in Philadelphia, she committed to the larger library to be named the Harry Elkins Widener Memorial Library. One room was to be set aside for Harry's collection. I had wanted to do it, but she wanted to do it herself. She commissioned the firm of her favorite architect Horace Trumbauer to build a library on the site of Gore Hall. Maybe this was her way of opening another door for herself after what she had been through.

At the 1913 Commencement, Nellie used a silver trowel to lay the cornerstone for the building. Two years later at the 1915 Commencement, the Library and the Memorial Rooms, opened. The keynote speaker was Henry Cabot Lodge, whose speech connected the war in Europe with Harry.

The pale marble and dark wood Memorial Rooms consist of an outer reception room, and the main room, which contains Harry's 3,500 books. His collection focuses on nineteenth century English literature, Shakespeare, and extra-illustrated books. Harry's particular favorites included the works of Robert Louis Stevenson and Charles Dickens as well as George, Isaac and Robert Cruikshank. The collection includes those that Harry purchased on that last trip to Europe and had sent home on another ship.

A London firm paneled the main room in carved English oak, which was put together in the United States. A huge portrait of Harry dominates the room, which is most appropriate. Harry loved his books. He would rummage around fusty old bookstores looking for forgotten literary treasures just as a treasure hunter looks for treasure. When he found a rare first edition, he'd say, "This is better than digging for gold." In my dreams, I often see him visiting the library late at night checking on his books, ensuring that his Stevenson and Dickens collections are there. In 1916, his mother requested that Harvard keep fresh flowers on the table by his photograph at all times.

One of the largest libraries in the United States, Widener has well over three million books and several miles of stacks. Looking out on grass and trees, the Beaux-Arts brick building is located on the south side of Harvard directly across from Memorial Church. It has a monumental pillared facade and a classical appearance. The printer's marks of Caxton, Rembolt, Fust, Schoeffer, and Aldus—all famous early printers—are carved over the center door. Harry would have liked that touch.

Of course, those Harvard students tell all sorts of stories. They say that Nellie required Harvard to serve ice cream (Harry's favorite dessert) in the dining halls and that all incoming students should pass a swim test: Had Harry learned to swim at Harvard instead of collecting books maybe he would have survived. I tell myself that even if had been able to swim, he couldn't have survived in such cold water.

I am getting old, but I still have the Gutenberg Bible I bought for Harry in my collection. When I hold it, I see Harry's face studying the beautiful illuminations and his hand stroking the cover. Of the two hundred Gutenberg Bibles printed between 1454 and 1456, this one is among the first ten. He would have cherished it. Maybe that's why I have held onto it...because I still see him enjoying his books.

Epilogue

After the death of the grandfather, the Bible, printed between 1450 and 1455, passed to Widener's uncle, Joseph. Following his death, Widener's brother and sister sent the Bible to the Widener collection because it "had been bought for Harry and should be among his books."

8

Chapter Eight:

Bon Appetit

Many of us have the ghost of Julia Child hovering over us in the kitchen. She taught us about making lentil or bean soups, chicken Kiev with a gush of herbal butter, Caesar salad — without anchovies, if you please, and the famous Gateau Saint-Honore. From her, we learned to use our senses, to enjoy our hunger.

When I was a young cook, I found her recipes too long, too detailed, but without them I would not have learned how to bone chicken breasts, open oysters, or clarify stock. Now that I am an aging cook, I find that Julia's raspy voice is still whispering in my ear as I deal with a complex sauce that is considering curdling or a potato cake that refuses to flip. She haunts my cooking, and it is the better for it.

††††††††††

When I married at age 21, my mother worried that I couldn't cook. "Now, Annette, you know you don't cook very well. And your Thomas might be quite unhappy when he tastes some of your meals."

My mother's food wasn't anything special, by the way. Each Sunday she cooked a Brahmin dinner: grey meat, mushy potatoes, and overdone vegetables. We ate the leftovers until at least Wednesday, and then she made a cream of mushroom soup casserole or a frosted meatloaf. Meals were not a thing of glory in our household.

"Mama, I know you believe that the way to a man's heart is through his stomach. And that I'm just going to upset my husband's stomach."

"I didn't say that, dear."

"But you came close."

I bought *Joy of Cooking* and began my culinary journey. The same year, 1963, WGBH (PBS, Boston) began broadcasting the "French Chef." Now for those of you who never watched Julia Child swooping, gasping, and clucking over her cooking demonstrations, you may not

Julia Child spent over forty years living, entertaining and cooking at this Cambridge address. In 2002, she donated her 14-by-20-foot kitchen, where she cooked for more than forty years and filmed several TV cooking shows, to the Smithsonian Institution, Washington D.C. The kitchen, along with more than 1,200 cooking gadgets is displayed in a permanent exhibition at the Smithsonian's National Museum of American History. *Courtesy of D. Peter Lund*

understand what an eye opener she was. Everyone loved her. On Wednesday nights when we heard the French Chef theme, we would stop whatever we were doing and take notes. All my friends watched her; we marveled that some of our husbands, including my Thomas, loved this tall, robust woman, who enthusiastically described what kind of electric mixer she was using or how to make galantine of turkey. She made cooking understandable and encouraged us to relax and trust our instincts. She showed us that if the chicken lands on the floor, how to dust it off and serve it with aplomb and without apology.

My cooking improved substantially. I learned how to deglaze a pan, beat egg whites, fold them into the soufflé to get the maximum puff, and sauté my meat so that it browned perfectly. Thanks to Julia, I can make an aromatic onion soup, a hearty coq au vin, and a wonderful mousse au chocolat. Thomas and I began to love fine cuisine. Out went my cans of cream of mushroom soup; in came capers, red wine, and salt-free butter.

From my viewpoint in the twenty-first century, I can see how much Julia Child radically changed American cuisine through her French cooking school, award-winning cookbooks, and world-renowned television programs—all three of which took place in Childs' home kitchen on 103 Irving Street, Cambridge. She was such a key figure in America's culinary history that her kitchen, which her husband designed with high counters to accommodate her formidable height, was donated to the Smithsonian National Museum of American History. Although many good chefs have followed in her footsteps, her ghost hovers over all of us as we try new techniques, work with gourmet ingredients and practice cooking as a creative endeavor.

When Thomas and I moved into our first apartment, we invited our parents to dinner. "Boeuf en Daube a la Provencale with little white turnips sautéed in butter," I announced proudly.

"What's that?" asked my non-traveled Mama.

"Braised pot roast of beef with wine, tomatoes, and Provencal flavorings."

"You cooked with wine?" She was aghast. Boston Brahmins in those days certainly didn't cook with wine. They barely even drank it.

"I did — just like Julia showed me."

"Julia who?"

"Julia Child. The French Chef."

"Is she very tall? With a warbly voice?"

"Yes. Why?"

"I went to Smith with her. We've been corresponding ever since. She mentioned something about a TV show." My mother sighed. "Her life is so much more exciting than mine."

"You know Julia? She's my idol."

"Certainly do. After we graduated in 1934, she went back to Pasadena until she decided to be a novelist or some sort of writer. Then she went to New York, but that didn't work out. So back she went to Pasadena. The rest of us were getting married and having babies, but she didn't meet anyone — of course, she was very tall — over six feet."

Mama fell silent. "She was what they call a late bloomer."

"So what happened?"

"The war. She went to Washington, D.C. Eventually, she got a job with the OSS, the Office of Strategic Services."

"Wasn't that the huge spy network created by President Franklin D. Roosevelt and the forerunner of today's CIA?" asked Thomas.

"Yes, and she worked directly with General William J. Donovan."

Thomas whistled. "Wild Bill Donovan. He's famous!"

"Yes, I think that's true, dear." Mama patted his hand. "In 1944, Julia sailed off to Ceylon, now known as Sri Lanka. She served as Chief of the OSS registry, which meant that she knew everything that was going on. So while I was changing diapers and preparing your Father's martini, she was dealing with wartime secrets, elephants, and potential invasions and at the same time meeting adventurous people who loved their cloak-and-dagger work. I envied her. There I was home with my apron on, cleaning pablum off the high chair, and she was sightseeing in China. During this time, Julia met the well-traveled, multilingual, sophisticated Paul Child, another OSS officer, who loved good food and music. She was much intrigued by Paul and his friends. Although she was ten years younger and several inches taller, they were attracted to each other. When both were assigned to China, they began a relationship. Paul introduced her to the joy of eating and the delight of talking about it. The war ended, however, and she returned to Pasadena, and he went back to Washington."

"Mama, you're telling a love story."

"Yes, I guess I am." She smiled happily. "She wrote me that her goal was to become Mrs. Paul Child — that was his name. She had decided she had to do something to catch her man because she was well on her way to being an old maid. She read the authors Paul suggested; then she turned to cooking, figuring that would bring her closer to him. She wrote me some funny stories. A duck blew up in her oven because she forgot to prick the skin — what a mess. She had sauces that congealed and soufflés that fell." Mama laughed. "Of course, I've never made a soufflé. Maybe I should watch her show too."

"Back to your story, please," urged Thomas.

"Did I tell you that this stew is delicious, dear?"

Dad harrumphed, "If your dessert is anywhere as good as this, I've died and gone to heaven."

"Well, let me get back to my story. They kept writing, and eventually Paul showed up in Pasadena. They drove back to Washington together. She was nearly thirty-four years old when they married. In 1948, the State Department assigned Paul to the United States Information Agency in Paris. I think that was when she fell in love with French cuisine."

"Why?"

"Well, she wrote me about her first meal. I think they began with oysters on the half shell. Paul ordered Sole Meunière. Julia wrote that it was perfectly browned in a sputtering butter sauce with a sprinkling of chopped parsley on top. She still recalls it as the most exciting meal of her life. (Julia Child and Alex Prud'homme, *My Life in France.*)

"Julia was at home in France. She took French lessons, walked the streets with her Michelin guide, learned about cheese, and sampled the wine. Finally, at age 37, she signed up to take cooking lessons with ex-GIs who were training to become restaurant chefs at one of France's most prestigious cooking schools, Le Cordon Bleu. She wrote about soufflés, galantines, ragouts, omelets, and mayonnaise. She tried out new dishes on her husband and friends, indulging in marathon amounts of butter and cream. She and two friends opened a cooking school, "L'Ecole des Trois Gourmandes," and began teaching French home cooking to American women in Paris. She saw that women — we didn't think about men cooking in those days — needed dependable recipes. Ten years later, she published her first book."

"I bet I know that book: *Mastering the Art of French Cooking."* I interrupted. "It's great. The recipes come together just as the instructions say they will. My cream puffs are no longer soggy."

"You make cream puffs?" queried Mama.

"Now that I met Julia, I do."

Mama laughed. "Funny to think of Julia as the French chef; her big culinary moment when we were at Smith was as chairwoman of the Refreshment Committee for the Senior Prom and Fall Dance. And now you're following her directions for cream puffs!"

Thomas leaned forward. "Before you get dessert, which is fantastic by the way, you need to tell us the rest of the story."

"In 1961, Julia and Paul returned to the States, settling in Cambridge. That's when she published her first book. It was an immediate critical and popular success. WGBH Boston asked Julia to try out a series of TV cooking shows, and the rest, as they say, is history! And her husband Paul helped make it all happen. They were a team!"

Mama sighed. "My big, gawky, basketball-playing college friend has become famous. Everyone knows her. Her books are considered critical masterpieces. And what have I done with my life?"

"Raised three children," Thomas replied, hugging her.

"Thank you, dear. Now where's that dessert?"

Mama died in 1990, but Julia continued building her legacy. The French Chef TV series succeeded in changing the way Americans related to food. Julia became TV's first food celebrity during the Kennedy Camelot years, when the country was becoming enamored with foreign travel and women's roles were expanding.

Her enthusiasm and can-do attitude made people feel that they, too, could be creative in the kitchen. After some two hundred television programs on classical French cooking, Julia explored contemporary cuisine in several more programs. The first woman inducted into the Culinary Institute Hall of Fame, Julia received France's highest honor, the Legion d'Honneur, in November 2000. In August 2002, the Smithsonian's National Museum of American History unveiled the exhibit featuring the kitchen where she filmed her popular cooking shows. She died in 2004.

I am quite sure wherever she is now, she is teaching others about the joy of cooking. Over the years, Julia has hovered over my cooking. She was the one who told me that cooks are made and I could learn to cook with the right instruction. The fact that I was married to someone who loves good food inspired me. "Bon courage," she would bid her audience.

"Courage," she whispers in my ear when my French bread doesn't rise or the brulee part of the crème brulee doesn't crisp up. "Courage," she says as I approach a large fish with head and tail yet to be removed. And I — well I have learned how to say "Bon appétit" with feeling.

9

Cambridge, Massachusetts

Chapter Nine:

The Bold Irish Girl

May the road rise up to meet you.
May the wind be always at your back.
May the sun shine warm upon your face;
The rains fall soft upon your fields and until
we meet again,
May God hold you in the palm of His hand.

Traditional Gaelic Blessing

††††††††††

Between 1820 and 1860, the Irish constituted over one third of all immigrants to the United States, and two-thirds of these Irish immigrants were Catholic. In the 1840s, as a result of the famine, nearly half of all immigrants to the United States came from Ireland.

In 1845, suddenly and silently, our potato crop failed. Not just ours...but *all* of Ireland's potato crop. Over four million people in Ireland depended on the potato as their chief food. The experts estimate that about one million died. Some died from starvation, but most people died of associated diseases such as dysentery and an outbreak of typhus. More than a million people fled Ireland. They risked their lives on long voyages aboard overcrowded ships to sail across the cruel sea to settle elsewhere — mainly in the United States, which promised them so many opportunities. With the failure of our potato crop, my life changed, but let me begin at the beginning...

I always had these lurid dreams. I can remember Ma waking me when I was little, saying, "Hush now, Margaret. You are only dreaming." But these weren't only dreams — they were frightening nightmares of dead people flung on the side of the road, of great waves, of a girl my age holding my hand, and the two of us laughing. When I told my Granny, she looked very thoughtful.

"What do you think, Granny?" I asked.

"I think you're thirteen going on fourteen, and you have second sight."

"I do?"

"Your dreams are trying to tell you something. They're lighting your way."

"To where?"

"That I don't know. We carry the past and future within us, in our bones. Your dreams are your destiny." She was confusing me. She confused me even further when she said, "You must live with a person to know a person. If you want to know yourself live with yourself."

The Potato and I

My family and I ate potatoes all the time. My family consists of ten of us. Pa and Ma, me at age 14, Thomas, age 12, Connor, 10, Sheila, 9, Maureen, 8, Kate, 7, David, 3, and baby Mary. It seems strange looking back now, but in those days, we ate potatoes morning, noon, and night, usually with buttermilk or tea. We would eat them toasted brown in the bottom of a heavy pot, mashed in milk, or with egg and butter. We would eat them boiled, peeling back the jacket and dipping the potato into a bowl of salt. Sometimes that was all we ate. To this day, potatoes mean comfort, family, and a thatched single-room cottage with a hard packed earth floor and a turf fire in the hearth.

Potatoes at morning
Potatoes at noon
And if I were to rise at midnight
Potatoes I'd get.

Nineteenth Century Children's Chant

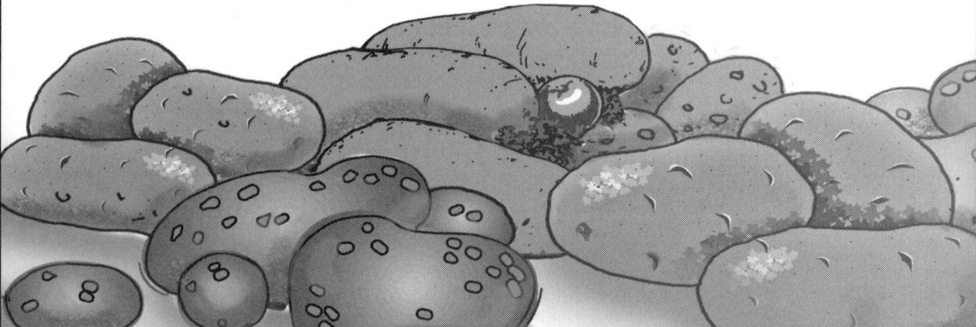

We lived in a small village outside Sligo, where several dozen one- and two-room thatch-roofed cabins clustered together. In the village, we had everything we needed: weavers, shoemakers, singers, musicians, and storytellers. In the long winter evenings, neighbors would gather by a fireside and tell stories of Ireland's past and sing those sad Irish songs, and the men folk would sip some whiskey. Pa once told me that the heat from the whiskey spread from the tips of his fingers down to the pit of his stomach, ending at the tips of his toes.

My father was a farmer who owned but a small spot of ground. He had a cow and some chickens and raised several good hogs out of an old sow each year. He grew potatoes and some wheat, which he sold to help pay the rent. My brothers helped him turn the earth with their spades and sowed the seed potatoes. I watched over my sisters as we tended the garden, scared birds away from the crops, and fed the pig, cow, and chickens. I did the wash and the sweeping out of our home. My ma would make the stirabout and oatcakes and tend to the babies. My granny would tell us stories about ghosts, fairies, and little people.

Then the famine came. Without potatoes, we were starving. Reluctantly, we ate our scrawny chickens, which meant no more eggs. Thomas and Connor would go to the river to search for crabs, winkles, and cockles. Sometimes they found a fluke. My sisters and I would head for the great meadows to seek out the button mushrooms, which came up overnight in small clusters of little white faces. We would look for nettles and blackberries, smudging our mouths and fingers purple while we filled our buckets to the brim. We did better than some of our neighbors because my brothers found bird eggs in the cliffs, and occasionally, during the winter, they were able to kill a bird or trap a rabbit. But we were still hungry. Little David suffered more than the rest of us; he had such thin little legs, and his eyes were so vacant. He looked like a little old man, all wrinkled and bent. By February, Pa butchered the cow because we had no food to feed her, but that meant we had no more milk. By April, we were eating old cabbage leaves, seaweed, and Indian corn. It was a long hard winter; then, Granny died from the bloody flux.

We planted our remaining seed potatoes and managed to get through the summer months as we waited for the harvest. My brothers trapped mice, rabbits, and birds. I took my little sisters out, and we walked forest and fields looking for edible roots and weeds. One day as I approached our home, I realized how desolate it was. No smoke curled up from the chimney. No hearth fire glowed orange through the windows. I found Ma just sitting with baby Mary in her arms. The poor little thing was so puny. She kept whining for something to eat. Ma would put Mary's lips to her breasts, but she had no milk. So Mary would keep on whining. I took Mary away from Ma and dribbled some water into her mouth to hush her. Pa came home and just sat silently. We were all waiting for the potato harvest.

Some couldn't wait; they roamed the countryside in search of food and work. We shared what we could and gave them a place to sleep besides our fire. In August, we had a heavy rain; the potato plants withered and blackened overnight. Even those that appeared healthy when Pa dug them up soon melted into a stinking rotten mess. Ma cried and cried. Pa visited his friends and came back stinking of whiskey. I kept my brothers and sisters away from him the next day.

One early September night, Pa disappeared for a long time. When he came home, he just sat in his chair with his head down. Finally, he raised his head. "We need to leave Ireland and find our fortune somewhere else." Little Maureen and Kate began to cry.

"I can't pay the rent. We don't have enough food. No one has food. My friend Patrick told me people are even eating their dogs and cats."

"What about the workhouse?"

"They bury you before you're dead there. They just throw you into a mass grave."

Thomas drew himself up, "I don't want to go to the workhouse." Mary began to wail, but Mom ignored her and pulled out her rosary beads instead.

"Neither do I," said Sheila.

Pa kept on talking. "People are getting sick and dying. The government tells us to bathe, to wear clean and comfortable clothing..."

"We don't have any. We sold anything we had," I replied.

"I know," he laughed bitterly. "And the officials tell us to eat wholesome nourishing meals."

Connor laughed, "Meals of what, Pa?"

Thomas added, "There isn't any food. We ate all the chickens. The cow is gone. We sold the hogs."

"But we have the sow still," Connor pointed out.

"The fields smell like death," I added quietly.

"We need to leave. We don't have any money to pay the rent. All I have left to sell is our old pig. And now the landlords' agents are throwing families into the street. They're tearing down the cottages and running the families off the land."

"Oh, Pa, that's awful."

"Indeed it is, Margaret. Our potato plants have blackened and withered. Any potato I dig out of the ground turns into black mush. There's not a single good potato left. We can't depend on you kids finding berries and crabs all year long. A man can't feed his family on that. We need to go to America," he said. "There's opportunity there, and there's nothing left here."

Ma began to sob. Sometimes I think she has cried everyday since baby Mary came. "There's no more food to feed my babies."

Pa went over to her and rubbed her shoulder. "Hush now, Peg. We still have the sow. I can sell her."

"And buy us passage?" I asked.

Thomas jumped up. "I've seen handbills promising plenty of work and good wages in America. The advertisements offer comfortable passage, economical fares ..."

Ma sobbed. Three-year-old David sucked his thumb; my younger sisters gathered around me.

"They say there's bread and work for all there," I said.

"And maybe the sun shines always there too," Ma said bitterly, bursting into noisy tears.

"Look, Peg," said Pa. "The potato crop has failed again. The cow and hogs are gone. We have nothing!" He banged his fist on the table. If we don't pay the rent, our landlord is going to evict us. We can leave Ireland or we can wait until we are evicted, and then we would have to find some sort of scalpeen to put over our head."

"Uncle Robert is doing well in Boston. Remember his letter, Ma?" I said. Ma was very fond of her younger brother.

Ma continued to sob in the corner.

"Why are you crying, my Peggy?" asked dad.

"Because I would be leaving everyone here."

"But they can come too. That's better than sitting here and starving. And we have family in Boston." Ma just kept on crying. She was worn out with the baby and my little brother. That night we ate our remaining turnips with some stirabout. The window was misted over with raindrops. Inside the air was thick with smoke from Pa's pipe and the peat burning in the fireplace.

I dreamt I was on a boat with many others. The waves were crashing against it. Then the boat was sinking, and I was hurling myself into the water. Crewmen began flinging chairs, baggage, and packing boxes at us — anything that could float. I started swimming towards a suitcase. Mary drowned. I was glad when morning came.

Pa and Thomas took the sow and went into town to sell her and get us tickets. Pa came back elated. "We have enough money to take a ship to Canada."

"But I thought we were going to Boston?" I said. "Uncle Robert is there."

"It's cheaper for us to go to Canada, and we only got so much for the sow. Then when we are there, we will make our way to Boston. I have some money hidden away." He hugged me. "We're going, Margaret! It's our chance."

Thomas was very quiet. When I asked him what was wrong, he began to cry. "I saw a dead man on the road's edge, Margaret. I don't want to die."

"We won't Tommy—we're going to America."

"Not all of us, Margaret. Pa says we're leaving Sheila and Maureen behind."

I stared at him. "Leaving them?"

"He says they can stay with Aunt Colleen while we find a home."

The night before we left, we prayed the rosary, ate what was left, drank, sang, and danced. The priest gave us a special blessing. My brothers were excited about our great adventure, but I wondered if I would ever see Sheila and Maureen again.

The Journey

The next morning, we loaded our belongings on to a handcart along with baby Mary and my brother David. Ma often had to sit in the cart; she was too tired. The rest of us walked alongside on the rocky path. As we walked, we passed little groups of people bearing coffins on their shoulder. We passed the dead — in the huts, the fields, on the roads. One dead woman had a baby at her breast. Poor and hungry like everyone else on the road, we just plodded along in silence.

We brought bedclothes, blankets, pillows, and utensils for eating and drinking. We had a supply of oaten cakes baked so much that they were hard as stones. We also had some eggs from my Aunt, which were rubbed with suet and bedded on their ends in salt to keep them edible.

While we were waiting for our ship, we stayed in a crowded boarding house where we slept six to a bed. I met Maggie there. She helped fill the gap that my sisters had left. She was about my age, and, of course, we were tickled she was Maggie and I was Margaret. Tossing her red curls, she said, "I'm on my own. I was the only one left at home, and then my Ma and Pa died from the Black Fever. I had nowhere to go. So I decided to emigrate!" I could almost feel my eyes bulging. Here, I had this big family, and she had nobody. She continued. "I heard that people can get rich in America, and I thought that sounded very nice." She laughed.

I agreed. "Definitely. Rich sounds good. Our landlord was rich, and his wife always had the most beautiful hats. Sometimes, she brought us small presents from England."

"You were lucky. I didn't get any fancy presents, but I could certainly do with having money." She scratched her arm.

"Someone told me that we are going to travel over 3,000 miles. We're going to be like these bugs...scratching out a living in a new land."

"I agreed." She scratched herself again. "I scratch all the time now. My ma used to say it's a bad hen that does not scratch herself." She picked off a louse.

"What are these?"

"They're lice. See this red dot? That's what their bite looks like."

"So what do I do?"

"Squeeze them so you kill them. And check your clothes." I sounded like my Granny, I thought.

Three days and many lice bites later, we were able to board our ship. Crewmen were hauling blocks and ropes; the sails were flapping in the wind. Peddlers were selling compasses and other equipment they said we would need aboard. "Look," shouted Maggie, "I can get a telescope so we can see our way."

I grabbed her hand firmly. "Don't you dare. They're just looking to take your last pennies from you. You'll need them on board."

Dock masters were giving orders. I could smell salty air and see large birds flapping overhead. What was really incredible was seeing all the pork, butter, eggs, and sides of ham sitting on the dock intended for the English people — food that the starving Irish people had grown to feed their rulers. "How can we be starving?" Maggie asked. "Look at all that food we're exporting." We hadn't seen that much food ever — except growing in the fields.

Tickets in hand, we joined the long line of Irish emigrants carrying their few bags and pots and pans for cooking. We were leaving our country of corpses and heading for a new land. We were aiming for Quebec, Canada, although Pa promised that we would head to Boston once we got there. "No more Union Jack. No King or Queen. We are going to have a President in the United States."

"Where's Boston?" asked Robert.

"It's south of Quebec, which makes it warmer."

"That's good."

"More importantly, it isn't British."

People were shouting out their goodbyes and "God Bless You." There was crying and laughing, excitement and confusion, sadness and the knowledge that we would probably never see Ireland or our friends and family here again.

Before boarding, a doctor asked to see our tongues as we passed him. Then crewmembers herded us like animals onto the crammed deck. I took baby Mary from Ma, who looked like she was going keel over. Someone behind me said we were on a coffin ship, which I found rather frightening. I hoped my younger sisters and brothers didn't hear the comment. When we pulled out, the spectators remaining on the dock cheered. We echoed their cheer.

In the 1840s, thousands of Irish immigrated to the United States to escape the widespread potato famine that haunted their country. Unlike earlier migrations, these people had few skills, no money, few clothes, and were desperately poor. Most had no education. As a result of the potato famine, nearly half of all immigrants to the United States originated from Ireland during this period. This sculpture entitled "The Great Hunger" is on the Cambridge Common. *Courtesy of D. Peter Lund*

Overhead, a flock of seagulls flew about. Ma began to moan as she realized that we would never see Ireland again. Thomas and Connor ran about with excitement. Maggie and I held hands. "To the future," we exclaimed. We had become best friends in our short time together; I never had time for friends before because I was always caring for all my brothers and sisters.

We spent the first day cruising down the river, borne along by the tide, before the river burst into the ocean. On deck we had our last glimpse of the green hills of Ireland. It all looked so peaceful. Who would guess that so many people were dying there?

The crowded and dirty steerage section was in the deepest hold of the ship, lit only by lanterns. It had little ventilation — none when the ocean was rough — and the hatches were shut and there was no room to move about. We slept side by side on narrow wooden bunks and foul, straw-stuffed mattresses. Luckily, I had a top bunk with Mary. It wasn't much fun to be on a bottom bunk if the people above you were seasick. The ceiling was only about five inches above me. The toilets for women were located at either end of the steerage section; men went above deck.

If anyone was sick in the dark, they had a hard time making it to the toilet. During the storms when the sailors battened down the hatches, and we were shut into steerage, people would shout, weep, and pray, "Help me, help me." I could hear the plea in their voices — their desperation and terror...and the shrieks of all their breaking hearts. The sea would seep in, timbers would creak, and people and baggage would get tossed about. One woman had her arm broken when a trunk slid into her. People yelled and screamed. It was bedlam.

The trip was supposed to take about forty days, depending on the prevailing winds, but in poor weather the crossing could take much longer. Our ticket promised that water would be doled out at the daily rate of six pints per passenger (children under age 14 would get half rations). It was to be used for cooking, drinking and washing. If the ship was delayed, our ration might be less. We were also supposed to receive one pound per day of flour, bread, rice, oatmeal, or potatoes and twice-weekly distributions of tea, sugar, and molasses. We had to provide any other water or provisions.

The provisions were not distributed as promised. Many of our fellow passengers — Maggie being one — had relied on the captain's observance of the promises contained in our tickets. After all, the price included payment for the weekly provision of food.

When it stormed the second night, the ship began to roll and pitch. We were flung back and forth in the pitch darkness. Through the sickening stench of bodies, blood, and urine, I heard moaning, shrieking, and chanting. Someone was shrieking that God was angry. The occasional flicker of light through the deck hatch told me whether it was daytime or night. I heard others vomiting and smelled vomit. I shut my eyes and dreamed of the smells and sights of my home. I heard the cows mooing in the field. They contentedly chewed their cuds as their great brown and white faces looked over towards our yard. I saw Thomas and me milking, and all of us having supper together. And before it was dark, we all knelt to say the rosary.

Another child died from dysentery. On a beautiful sunny day, the child was sewn up in cloth, along with a great stone, and flung into the sea. So far five people had died within twenty-four hours. Ma seemed to be doing poorly. When she walked, she tottered along. Her eyes were wild and hollow, and she paid little attention to anyone other than baby Mary, who looked all bones and eyes.

We were so crowded that many soon had ship fever from the body lice, diarrhea, and dysentery. When the hatches were open, we could go on deck in small groups. It was so good to get away from the terrible stench below. Connor was so excited when we saw a whale, although the crewmembers told us they were considered bad luck. Often sharks would follow our ship in the hope of finding a tasty morsel. In the first week, there were only a few deaths, but then the numbers began increasing. The bodies were wrapped in sailcloth and thrown overboard. Leaving beautiful green Ireland was hard. Children would ask for food from their mothers, who had none to give; men and women would groan or pray. When I wanted to cry, I went to Maggie. We supported each other.

Maggie was a great storyteller. She would keep me and the others amused often. One day my sisters and I crowded around her in the stinking steerage and she told a story that was almost as good as my Granny's stories. "One day," she said, "My friend Tom saw a Leprechaun with a pitcher of something. You know they say a body must never take their eyes off them, or they'll escape. So Tom kept watching the little man and finally he spoke to him. "May be you'd tell us what you've got in the pitcher there?" said Tom.

"That I will, with pleasure," said the Leprechaun. "It's good beer. I know because I made it myself. Would you like a taste?"

"Of course," Tom drank deeply, smacking his lips, "but I want even more a crock of your gold."

"So follow me," said the little man. "Come along with me, and I'll show you a crock of gold," said the Leprechaun. "You know Money swore an oath that nobody who did not love it should ever have it."

So off they went. Afraid that he would disappear, Tom held the Leprechaun tightly as they crossed the fields. Finally, they came to a great field full of cabbages. The Leprechaun pointed to a big cabbage, saying, and "Dig under that one, and you'll get your crock full of gold."

"I need a drink first," said Tom. Then he realized he didn't have a spade for digging. After another drink from the jug, he took off one of his red garters and tied it round the cabbage. He said to the Leprechaun, "Swear you'll not take that garter away from that cabbage." And the Leprechaun swore that he wouldn't touch it.

"I suppose," said the Leprechaun, very civilly, "you have no further occasion for me?"

"No," says Tom, "you may go away now, if you please. God speed you, and may good luck attend you wherever you go. But first give me one last drink."

"Of course and good-bye to you, Tom," said the Leprechaun.

"So Tom ran for home and got a spade, but he was so tired after all that drink that he sat and napped before returning to the field of cabbages. When he finally got there, every cabbage in the field had a red garter tied about it. So Tom realized that it is sweet to drink but much can be lost while drinking."

"Good story, Maggie," I said.

"But it's just a story. You know when we get there, we will have to find work. I think I want to be what they call a Bridget."

"What's that?"

"A maid. That way I will get room and board and some money. I'll also learn how to act and live here in America. And then I will meet a man..."

"I know. You will meet the handsome son of the family. He will dress you in velvet and feed you roast lamb and..."

"I'll live happily ever after."

"And you will have a coach and four and three maids."

"And a butler! I've always wanted a butler."

When the ocean was rough, the water poured into the hold where we lay. We encountered a severe storm and had to stay in steerage for almost three days. The sewage and filth washed around our bodies, which were rubbed raw by the wooden berths. We couldn't stand because there was no room. We were down in steerage all that time with the only light coming from the hatch opening. I knew from the sounds of retching that someone near me was very sick. The smell surrounded me like a fog.

Finally, they opened the hatch. The storm was over. The sun shone again.

As I clambered to the deck, blinded by the sun, Maggie approached me. "Do you know that prayer that says...

May God give you...
For every storm, a rainbow,
For every tear, a smile,
For every care, a promise,
And a blessing in each trial.
For every problem life sends,
A faithful friend to share.

"Yes, my Granny used to say that."

"Well, I said that to myself last night, and I thought of you."

I hugged her. Friends are wonderful.

"People died last night, Margaret."

"Where are their bodies?"

She pointed at the ocean. "I heard the sailors moving around early this morning and some great splashing."

Thomas came up behind us. "Maybe that means more food for us."

"Hush, Tom. That's a terrible thing to think," I reprimanded him. But when I looked at him, I saw the sunken eyes, the almost white lips, and the protruding bones. We were all hungry. Ma just shivered and stared into the distance. The baby had stopped crying. Pa was off with the men talking about what they would do in America. Sometimes the men seemed to do a lot of talking and not a lot of doing.

Attracted by the smell of food, people hung around the fireplaces upon either side of the foredeck. These fireplaces were large wooden cases lined with bricks, where we could cook our food. Many passengers just ate their food raw rather than waiting in line to take turns using the fireplace. Others bickered, prayed, or just stood in line. Some made porridge; some heated oatcakes that had been cooked back home. Our main meal consisted of herring and potatoes. If there was any wind or an argument between passengers, the ship's captain ordered that the flames be doused. So all those who had been waiting in line were left with cold or raw food.

People got sick and died everyday. Some women looked like they were almost dead. Young boys were hollow-eyed and decrepit. Baby Mary had died on the fifteenth day of the voyage. I gave away her clothes to a woman who asked for them. A crewmember put her in a canvas sack, and we said our goodbyes to her before they flung her overboard. Sharks were following the ship waiting for our loved ones. Maggie and I would sit on the deck, look at the waves, and talk about how it would be in America. She was determined to become a ladies' maid in a large elegant house. She wanted to wear a uniform, say "Yes, M'am," and save her money. I wasn't sure what I wanted.

Ma just lay in her berth, looking like a specter and wincing at the light. She no longer made any sense. Pa said he couldn't do anything about it and suggested that we all hold onto her and say the rosary. We did, but she didn't seem to hear us. Little Kate and David were looking poorly. Their eyes were large dark pools, and they couldn't seem to walk a straight line. I was afraid they would fall overboard.

At night, the number of bodies prevented any movement. People groaned, and I felt the spray of vomit from the woman on my left side. The girl on my right side told me that she had heard that one ship had caught on fire. So great was the heat that women jumped overboard with their babies in their arms.

I shut my eyes and eliminated my physical surroundings in my mind. I felt as if I was floating, weightless. I wasn't aware of the smell, the noise, the heat, or the dirt. I was nestled in my own world. Safe. Free. I saw my sisters Sheila and Maureen back in Ireland and wondered how they were. Faces floated into my mind: people from the past and present, a procession of silent images. Then the dream changed. The road signs were written in a different language, and I felt alone. I was like a stranger in a strange land.

When I woke up, I realized I wasn't alone. I had my friend Maggie. I had lost many things in the past months, but I had gained something truly important: a friend on this dreadful ship that was running out of food supplies. People had the bloody flux and the "itch" from lice. Medical help was nonexistent, and the noise and smells of steerage were horrendous, but I had a friend.

Somehow we enjoyed ourselves. Maggie told stories. An Irish fiddler would play, and we would dance on deck. And of course, we sang all those Irish songs. The women would sew and knit, and we would talk about our future.

Maggie had a rash. I promised her that despite my family I would stay by her. We pledged ourselves to believe in this new land and a fresh start.

When we began seeing birds, a sailor said we had entered the Gulf of St. Lawrence. People thronged the deck, shouting "Glory to God" or falling on their knees to pray the rosary. A straw-hatted inspector boarded. "Ha, there's fever here," he shouted. We sailed up the river to Grosse Isle, the quarantine island. About ten immigrant ships were anchored there, waiting to be inspected. A stream of small boats carried emigrants to shore. Walking was hard after all that time on the ship. Many crawled to the hospital. On the ship next to us, the crewmen were lifting the dead out of the hold with big hooks and stacking them like firewood.

Ma and David were just lying on a berth. I tried to keep them clean, but there was little water. Finally, Pa brought a nurse to us. She shook her head when she saw them. She looked up at my father, "They have typhus, you know. I don't think they will make it." Pa looked stricken. Then he said, "Do what you can," and he strode off with a frozen look on his face.

The doctor pulled Maggie out of line. "You can't go on until you get better. You have typhus." They put her in a small shed, where she lay with eight others. The rash crawled over her body; her eyes glittered with fever. I held her hand.

"Don't you go crying now, Margaret," she said. "If I don't make it, I'll still be with you. Don't you dare stand at my grave and weep. Remember the poem?

I am not there.
I do not sleep.
I am the thousand winds that blow!
I am the diamond glints on snow...
I am the sunlight on ripened grain...
I am the gentle autumn rain.
When you waken in the morning's hush,
I am the swift uplifting rush
Of gentle birds in circling flight...
I am the soft star that shines at night.
Do not stand at my grave and cry–
I am not there... I did not die...
I will still be with you.

Ma, David, and Maggie died and went into the same mass grave. My first real friend had wanted to find a fortune in America but all she found was a grave.

Although I knew that it made no sense, I was glad that they had each other. Maggie could certainly take care of Ma and David.

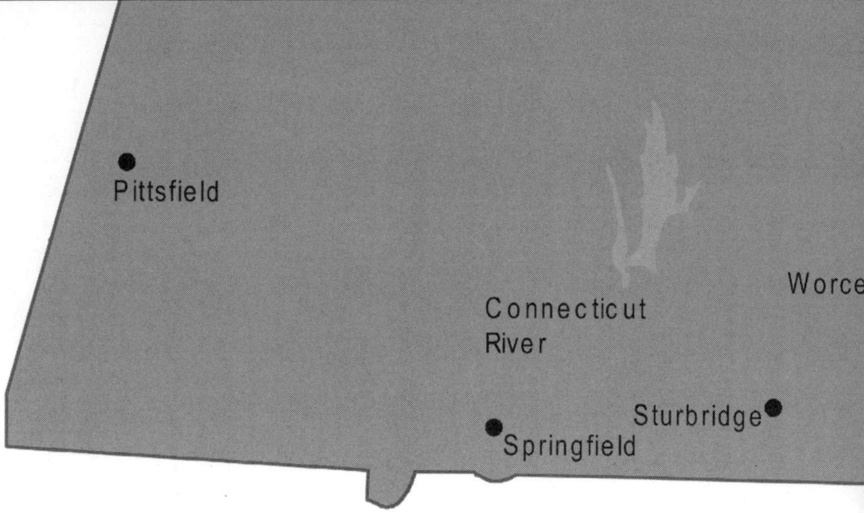

A New Country

As we traveled to Boston by foot and aboard a fishing vessel from Nova Scotia, I kept hearing Maggie telling me that I needed to establish a home and find work — that if I went into domestic work I'd get high pay, secure work, and a place to live.

The waterfront was a crowded, busy place with draft horses pulling wagons filled with goods to and from the brick warehouses; beaver-hatted men sporting blue tailcoats and black socks walked to and from their counting houses; grimy urchins ran about looking for work or spare coins. Our uncle lived in Cambridge near the river. He worked at the massive brickyard between Massachusetts Avenue and Alewife Brook. We moved in with him in a shack tucked into a nook in an alley. Other tenements, pigsties, horse stalls, and one overflowing privy surrounded us. The place had no light and little air. It reminded me of steerage. I had escaped from that, I told myself, so I could escape from here.

My uncle said, "It will be hard to get a job. You will have to take whatever work you can get."

"I thought this was the land of plenty," wailed Connor.

"Plenty if you're not Irish Catholic. You'll take the jobs that the others don't want."

"What if I don't want to?" Pa hit him, and he hushed.

My uncle said, "Many employers refuse to hire the Irish. They put signs in their windows and advertisements that read "NINA," which means, "No Irish Need Apply."

Pa said, "My back and shoulders are my livelihood. We have come too far not to get a job. We will get work."

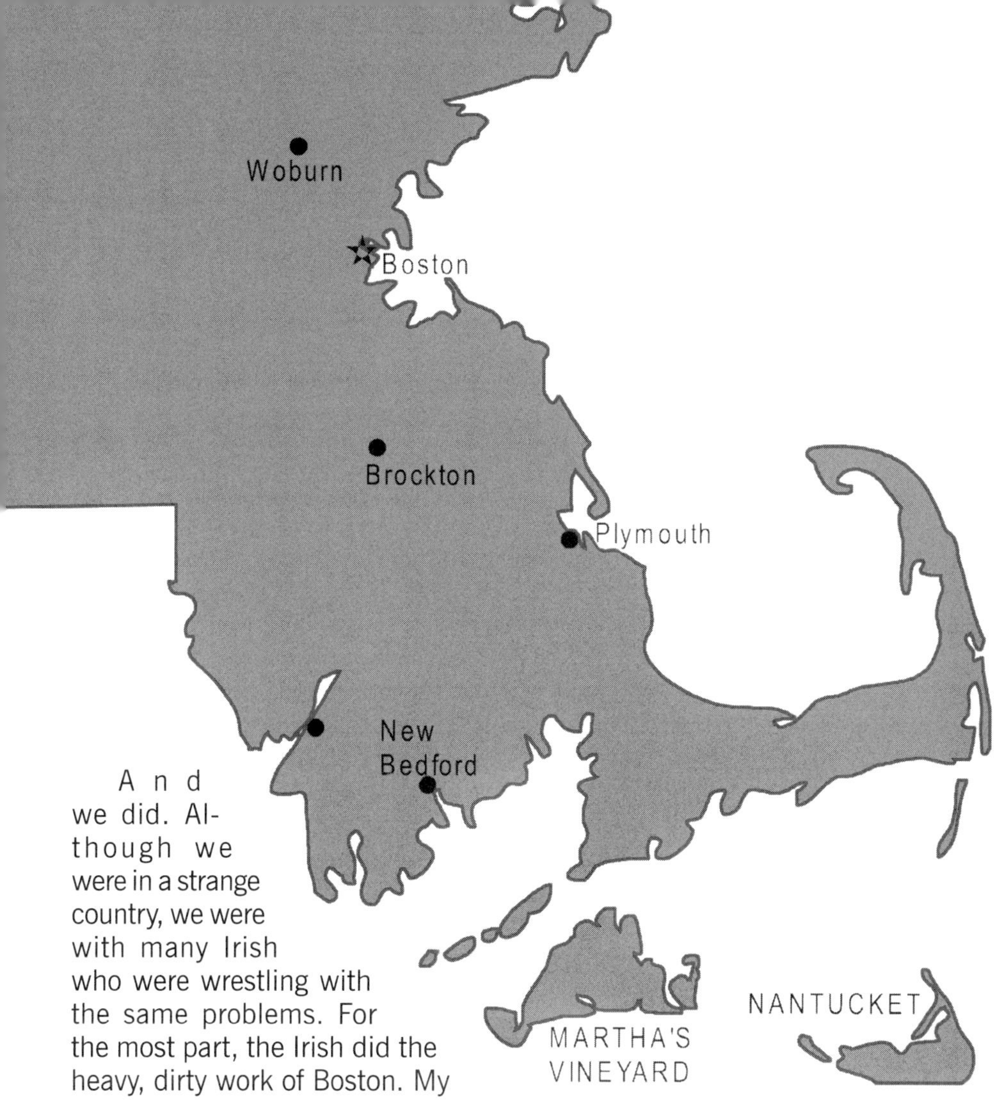

And we did. Although we were in a strange country, we were with many Irish who were wrestling with the same problems. For the most part, the Irish did the heavy, dirty work of Boston. My brothers and Pa could have been bricklayers, masons, carpenters, or plasterers if they had those skills, but they didn't. Instead, Pa became a laborer who did the digging and laying of pipes for the city. With his big smile, Connor quickly talked his way into sweeping the floors of the neighboring saloon, and Thomas shoveled up horse droppings from the streets. On Friday nights, they would pool their earnings and give me some money for food. We all lived with my uncle in a single room, without a window, that stank from the kerosene stove that I used for cooking, heating, and ironing. I took care of Katie and the cooking, laundry, and what cleaning there was, thinking I was too young to play Ma.

Then Katie died. We didn't really know what she died of. She was happily playing, and then she began vomiting. Within hours she was dead. Now my large family was reduced to just Pa, Thomas, Connor, and me.

I became a maid in an upper class Yankee household in a large elegant house. There was no handsome son, but I liked the excitement of their family gatherings. Below the stairs, we had fun, and I made friends. Despite my Romanism, my employer respected me. When I asked for Sunday to be my day off so I could go to Mass, they hesitated, but they gave it to me. I labored nearly twelve hours per day, six and half days per week, for an average weekly wage of $3.99, including room and board. I learned how to polish brass and silver, make tea sandwiches, shop in America, and cook the best of foods. Each month I sent some money home to my Aunt Colleen for Sheila and Maureen.

Occasionally, Maggie would nudge me in the middle of the night. She would tell me that I could make it in this new world. In the morning, I would resolve again to have my own home and my own family.

Now that they were eating again, Thomas and Connor were working in construction. They had long hours; they were known as shanty Irish, but they were making money. They complained about Pa, who would drink too much. Sometimes his friends would bring him home. And sometimes he didn't come home. He used his fists on Thomas and Connor sometimes, but he left me alone.

I tried talking to him, but my stalwart Pa had disappeared. Now he was saying such things as, "It is a serious moment in a man's life when he says farewell to beautiful Ireland forever. We took a perilous voyage, to be sure, Margaret, and we watched our loved ones die."

"Yes, Pa, but we're still alive, and we're making a living here. And Sheila and Maureen are still alive in Ireland."

"That doesn't suffice."

At church, I met tall and brawny Thomas McCarthy, a strong, tall ice cutter. He worked with Mr. Tudor harvesting ice in Fresh Pond to be shipped as far as India. He asked Pa for my hand before I knew he was going to ask me. We married in October. It's as they say, "If in October you do marry Love will come but riches tarry." We had few riches, but lots of love until he died.

We had four American children who lived. As I raised them, I told them Irish stories and sang them those melancholy Irish songs. I told them that education, a good appearance, and good manners would carry them a long way. I told them about the days in Ireland, the ship, and my friend Maggie. I told them that they were Americans — that they could do anything in this marvelous country if only they worked for it. No one was going to give them a pot of gold for nothing. They had to use their own brains to get it. And I told them the stories that Maggie had told me. They liked best of all the story of the Leprechaun.

They all finished school and had good lives. My oldest, Patrick, ventured west to mine gold in California. My second Neil worked on the Northern Pacific Railroad in Dakota Territory. I worried about him the most because laborers had to blast tunnels through rock and the rugged terrain. They say that an Irishman was buried under every American railroad tie, but to the best of my knowledge he survived. My other two children stayed in Cambridge. James, who had been my religious one, became a priest, and my Maggie became a nurse. Now, she is getting married to a banker, who wants to own a turreted, towered, multi-chimney home on a large green grass square outside of the city. He says that their new home will have room for me, and I can take care of their babies. In the night, my faithful friend Maggie smiles and hugs me.

Part Three:

Lore

In ages past, our old ones were the storytellers. Folks sat around the supper table and shared stories with each other. Their tales were part of our heritage. They were ones we all know — that we have grown up with. Many of the following stories were created in the twentieth century when our parents attended those famous Cambridge universities.

Chapter Ten:

The Academic Pit Stop

Many American universities have proud traditions based around college pranks. Even in the early eighteenth century, when Harvard College applicants had to be well versed in Greek or Latin and cows roamed the Yard, Harvard students were guilty of shenanigans. Then, as now, they had food fights or they would provoke their tutors through tomfoolery.

Some professors could handle these students. A story is told about Harvard's first president, Henry Dunster, who, while visiting a relative, was told that he was urgently needed back at Cambridge. "The scholars had raised the devil!" according to the messenger. In those grim Puritanical days, the Devil was highly feared. President Dunster returned quickly to Cambridge, where he found the college in an uproar. Some of the scholars had dabbed in black magic, he was told, and the Devil had appeared. The younger students were thoroughly terrified. A quick-witted man, President Dunster donned his exorcist role and, with a certain amount of fanfare, emptied his gunpowder horn in the Yard. He laid a train, lit it with a live coal, and literally "Blew the Devil out of Harvard College."

Harvard College History

In 1636, The Great and General Court of the Massachusetts Bay Colony (the Massachusetts legislature at that time) decreed that a college should be built "in the Wilderness" and granted £400 (more than half the tax levy for the entire colony that year) towards its construction. By building a "New College" in the New World, the Puritans would not have to send their sons back to England for an education. Their objective was to have the college train church, state, and business leaders for the colony.

Harvard University celebrated its 350th anniversary in 1986. Several other universities claim to be the oldest; however, Harvard is acknowledged as the oldest institution of higher learning in the

United States. Although there are older universities throughout the world, what is amazing is that this world-renown university was founded in 1636 — only six years after the founding of Boston and Cambridge and sixteen years after the *Mayflower* arrived in Plymouth. Those strong-minded Puritans may have lacked many of the niceties that they had had in their lives in England, but they fervently believed in the importance of education to further "purify" the church and perfect social living. They saw the establishment of the college as essential to their life in the New World despite the hardships of pioneer life.

Only two years after the college's founding, John Harvard, a young minister, died of consumption at age 30. He left half his estate and his library to the new college.

††††††††††

In November 1607, John Harvard, the son of a butcher, was born in St. Saviour's Parish, Southwark, England near London Bridge. His father and four of his five siblings died in the 1625 plague. His mother then married a prosperous cooper, who died soon after, leaving the Harvard family well to do.

Harvard studied at Emmanuel College, Cambridge, where he earned an A.B. in 1631 and an A.M. in 1635. Although Harvard received religious training, he did not appear to have been ordained to the ministry nor was he connected officially with any church.

In July 1635, Harvard's mother died following a third marriage; his brother also died. Harvard inherited from both of them and married Anne Sadler, a classmate's sister. After selling four inherited houses and purchasing a large number of books, they immigrated to America in 1637 and settled in Charlestown, Massachusetts, where they joined the Puritan Church. John served as the assistant to the pastor of the First Church of Charlestown and as a teaching elder, which required him to explain scripture and deliver sermons to the congregation. Then he became ill. Some say that as he lay dying, he muttered, "Give my books (he had a library of approximately four hundred volumes) and half my estate to the College; the rest goes to my beloved wife." He died in Charlestown September 14, 1638.

The amount of Harvard's bequest has never been officially determined because much of his estate consisted of real estate in England, which was not readily converted to cash. His bequest provided enough money to construct a sizeable building first known as Harvard College and then later known as Harvard Hall.

His bequest stimulated others, including Lady Mowlson, Anne Radcliffe, in 1643, to make further bequests, securing the future of the new college. On March 13, 1638, The Great and General Court ordered that the college should be called Harvard College in honor of its earliest benefactor.

John's Statue Erected

In 1884, Daniel Chester French, an MIT dropout who received an honorary Harvard degree in 1917, sculpted the statue of John Harvard, which sits prominently in Harvard Yard in front of University Hall. The gift of Samuel James Bridges, it stood originally in the delta west of Memorial Hall, but in 1924 it was moved to its present location in the Yard. Some have conjectured that the move was in order to keep all light out of the Dean's office!

A large crowd assembled in Sanders Theatre for the debut of the statue on October 15, 1884. The gathering included President Eliot, the sculptor French, and Samuel J. Bridge, donor of the statue, who had received an honorary degree in 1880. The statue reportedly cost over $20,000. The crowd watched the unveiling and, according to accounts in *The Harvard Crimson,* "gave three cheers apiece for John Harvard, Samuel Bridge and Daniel French."

Pit Stop and Hoops

Harvard tour guides refer to the handsome bronze statue as *the statue of three lies,* because of its inscription, "John Harvard, Founder, 1638."

† Lie 1: The model for the statue was a member of the class of 1882 dressed in Puritan garb — not John Harvard, who died long before it was sculpted. John Harvard left no portraits of himself.
† Lie 2: The University was already in existence when John Harvard died.
† Lie 3: The University was established in 1636.

According to the December 18, 2006, *Harvard Crimson*, John Harvard's statue enjoys a fascinating role on campus. Throughout the day, busloads of tourists come to stand before him like pilgrims to Rome. Awestruck, they take their pictures with him. They rub

Tourists rub the statue's foot for good luck—so much so that the statue's bronze foot shines in the sun. Unfortunately, Harvard students are rumored to urinate on the very foot that tourists rub for good luck. *Courtesy of Siobhan Theriault*

In 1924, Harvard President A. Lawrence Lowell organized the move of the John Harvard statue, sculpted by Daniel Chester French in 1884, to a prominent site fronting University Hall.
Courtesy of Siobhan Theriault

the famously shiny foot for good luck and hope that they too will attain their utmost desire.

Unfortunately, Harvard students are rumored to urinate on the very foot that tourists rub for good luck. From the moment the sun sets, according to the *Crimson*, students are said to pee upon him. This famous statue sculpted by the same man who created the Abraham Lincoln Memorial in Washington, D.C. is "Harvard's favorite late-night pit stop."

All night, students urinate on this monument to higher education in America.

The bronze statue of John Harvard has suffered other humiliations as well.

One famous prank involved Wellesley College women, who often date Harvard College men. Each May Day, Wellesley women greet the spring by a hoop rolling race, where they push metal hoops along with a stick. During the 1930s, people thought that the hoop-rolling winner would be the first person in her class to be married.

In 1939, disguised as a Wellesley student in a blue skirt, white blouse, saddle shoes, and red wig, Edward Cameron Kirk Read, president of the *Harvard Lampoon*, hid himself in some bushes on the race route. As the 400-plus Wellesley girls raced by, Read joined in. He won the race and was presented with a bridal bouquet of sweet peas. He said he was engaged to a Harvard man, but his wig became askew and his true masculine voice overpowered his feminine tones. Horrified, the Wellesley women dragged him to Lake Waban and tossed him in.

Jealous that they had not conceived of the prank themselves, *Harvard Crimson* photographers kidnapped Read and photographed him bound and gagged, which was subsequently printed on the front page of the *Boston Globe*. *The Lampoon* retaliated by kidnapping three *Crimson* editors and supposedly hung them from meat hooks in a refrigerator. According to the *Crimson* (Friday, May 05, 1939), Wellesley "girls were discovered clambering over the University Hall statue (of John Harvard) in the rosy hour before dawn." Poor John was wearing a Wellesley gown, a Wellesley banner, and a large violet "W." As the piece de resistance, they encircled his shoulders with a hoop!

After Ned Read's adventure, men from a number of schools competed with each other to run as the imposter male in the annual race and to be thrown into the lake. It became an honor of sorts, as the male "winner" was featured alongside the Wellesley winner in newspapers across the nation. The hoop rolling itself continues to make syndicated news wires.

Pranks & Hacks

On November 20, 1992, three Yale undergraduates and a Harvard graduate student, who graduated from Yale, were found climbing on the statue. They had a paint can; blue paint covered their clothes; and the blue paint on the statue was still wet. The security guard declared he had caught them "Blue handed." The statue has been painted a Dartmouth green, coated with tar, decorated with protest banners in the 1960s, and adorned with banana peels.

In 1933, the *Crimson r*eported that before the Harvard/Yale game members of the *Lampoon* kidnapped Handsome Dan II, the Yale mascot. Later on, he was seen licking meat rubbed on the feet of the John Harvard statue.

In 1960, MIT hackers placed a toilet stall door in front of the statue. It advertised "Johnny on-the-Spot, Portable Toilets, Rented/Serviced, Boston, Mass. Capital 7-0777."

One Sunday, after Harvard lost to Yale in 1990, a group of MIT hackers wandered into Harvard Yard. They wrapped a cast around the statue's right leg, placed a skull cap on its head, and encircled its neck with an "MIT Medical Department" neck brace decorated with a pin that said "ask me about my lobotomy."

When the media aired the news that Unibomber Ted Kaczynski was a 1962 Harvard graduate, MIT hackers outfitted the statue with wild hair, mustache, and sunglasses and dressed him in a white hooded sweatshirt and a pair of handcuffs. Thanks to their fashion design, John resembled the FBI mug shot of Kaczynski.

More recently, prior to a heavily advertised video game being released, MIT hackers transformed the statue of John Harvard into a genetically engineered soldier and savior of the universe. They stuck a helmet on the statue's head, tucked a toy assault rifle into the crook of his arm and then bragged about their handiwork on the hacks.mit.edu website. He had become a video game superhero!

11

Chapter Eleven:

Something Fishy

When the Massachusetts legislature paraded from the Old State House at the corner of State and Washington Streets to the new Bulfinch-designed State House one-quarter mile away at the top of Beacon Hill in 1895, they carried a four-foot, eleven-inch carved fish wrapped in an American flag. They hung it above the entrance to the hall in the Visitors Gallery inside the chamber of the House of Representatives. When the house is meeting, the speaker of the house faces the cod. It is said that the head of the cod points at whichever party is currently in power.

The "Sacred Cod" symbolizes how much the humble cod fish means to the Commonwealth. Without it, Massachusetts' survival and success wouldn't have been so easy. Of course, any emblem of civic pride — especially a fishy item — can incite college pranksters. In 1933, the *Harvard Lampoon* staff decided they had to possess that Sacred Cod. They knew that to succeed in obtaining it they had to divert their archrival, *The Harvard Crimson*, which never missed an opportunity to sabotage the *Lampoon*'s plans. Therefore, *The Crimson* had to be sidetracked. To that end, the *Lampoon* editors created a distraction by raiding the *Crimson* offices and kidnapping a staff member. This action infuriated the other *Crimson* staffers, who promptly focused all their attention on locating the missing staff member.

Having successfully sidetracked the potential saboteurs, several *Lampoon* staffers walked into the State House armed with a pair of wire cutters and a long flower box. Once the tourists disappeared, they quickly cut the wires holding up the fish, tucked their piscine trophy in the box, and disappeared.

The Search for the Cod

An anonymous call alerted reporters that the cod was gone. The theft of the famous fishy icon, which had hung in the State House since 1799, became front page news. Reporters used their most florid prose as they trawled for hints. Even Los Angeles newspapers cast a line or two. State police were called in to assist with the search. Resentful policemen dragged the Charles River basin.

State legislators were unsure about returning to session without their Sacred Cod, but they decided to convene anyway. Speaker Saltonstall is said to have gazed mournfully at the spot where the silvery fish used to hang as he began the session. Although other pressing matters loomed on their agenda, the legislators spent the day debating about the penalties that they could bring to bear on the culprits.

For two days the police raced around the city following fishy leads. One tip told them that the cod was located in an MIT basement. The police found a large box containing only a tiny sardine!

Suspicion focused on the *Lampoon* because bystanders at the State House had seen a group of young men wearing white saddle sport shoes, which Harvard students wore in the 1930s. Someone else remembered a young man walking away carrying a long florist box. The culprits had to be *The Lampoon*, the police figured, but *Lampoon* staff members denied their involvement.

The Cod Restored

In its April 28, 1933, issue, The *New York Times* reported that the *Harvard Crimson* asserted that members of the staff of the *Harvard Lampoon* had stolen the "Sacred Cod" from its shrine in the Gallery of the House of Representatives.

Finally, on the night of April 28, the Superintendent of Harvard Yard received an anonymous tip informing him that if he wanted to retrieve the Sacred Cod, he should go to the West Roxbury Parkway and follow an unlicensed car. This angle seemed worthwhile. Dutifully following the tipster's instructions, the Superintendent followed in the car's wake and was gratified when it pulled off the road. Two young men, with their faces concealed, handed him the cod.

Imagine his delight! The Commonwealth of Massachusetts had been adrift for fifty hours while the Sacred Cod had gone aground. The Superintendent immediately returned the cod to the House of Representatives, where it was hung six inches higher to prevent any future pranks. Subsequently, the Superintendent was promoted to head of Harvard security.

Incidentally, the Massachusetts Senate also has its own sacred fish; it's known as the "Holy Mackerel."

12

Cambridge, Massachusetts

Chapter Twelve:

The Ibis and the Cold War

In the middle of Harvard Square amid all those columned brick buildings sits the flat-ironed Lampoon Building on a triangular sidewalk spit. Designed by E. M. Wheelwright, the small, three-storied mock-Flemish castle has emblazoned wooden doors and leaded glass windows. On its pointed roof stands the *Lampoon*'s mascot, a copper Ibis, which is frequently stolen. The *Rolling Stone Magazine* ranked one of its many thefts as the Number 1 prank of the twentieth century.

In 1953, Dwight D. Eisenhower was sworn in as U.S. President, and Nikita Khrushchev was named First Secretary of the Communist Party when Joseph Stalin died. Although the United States and the Soviet Union had never declared war, the two superpowers had been engaging in military buildup and political battles for support around the world since the end of World War II. The United States sought the "containment" and "rollback" of Communism and embarked on a foreign policy around this goal, while the Soviet Union fostered worldwide Communist movements. As Cold War tensions escalated, Republican Senator Joseph McCarthy, from Wisconsin initiated his muckraking efforts to rid the United States of Communist sympathizers. Meanwhile, the press lambasted Harvard as the Kremlin on the Charles and accused it of being a hotbed of Communism.

During this period, *Crimson* staffers, Michael Maccoby, David Halberstam (the future Pulitzer Prize journalist), and George Abrams stole the sacred Ibis from the rooftop of their rival, the *Lampoon*. The day after the theft, the *Crimson*, Harvard's daily student newspaper, printed a photo of the Ibis with the headline announcing, "Upset Updike Wants the Bird." In retaliation, the *Lampoon,* led by its then-president John Updike kidnapped *Crimson* staffer Maccoby. In keeping with Cold War diplomacy, the staff members of the warring newspapers met on a bridge spanning the Charles River presumably to exchange Maccoby for the Ibis. The *Crimsonians*, however, double-

NO
STOPPING
ANYTIME
HR
PARKING

crossed them and fled south with both Maccoby and the Ibis—and with *Lampoon* staff members in hot pursuit.

Arriving in New York, the *Crimson* staff members announced that Harvard was donating the treasured Ibis to the new Moscow State University. They expressed their hope that it would perch on a Russian spire as a "symbol of the universality of the search for truth," recalls George S. Abrams '54, then managing editor of the *Crimson*. Accepting the offer, Semyon Tsarapkin, Russia's deputy ambassador to the United Nations, was said to be visibly touched when presented with the Ibis. One small problem was that many pigeons had roosted on it, leaving their marks behind (*Crimson*, June 07, 2004) and the ambassador somewhat befouled!

The presentation of the gift occurred under a portrait of Vladimir I. Lenin, with Harvard student and photographer, John Loengard, capturing the moment for posterity. The photos were quickly disseminated to major news sources such as *Life Magazine*. According to the *Crimson*, on April 21, 1953, Abrams and Maccoby said, "The Russians were extremely nice about the whole thing. It seemed to us they were going out of their way to implement their new peace offensive. We expect to get pictures from them of the Ibis' new resting place on a University of Moscow spire almost any day now."

The *Crimson* also stated, "Tsarapkin was a bit puzzled as to what the bird represented. First he thought it was a stork but was assured when he was informed it was a sort of American peace dove."

M. Wheelwright designed the flat-ironed Lampoon Building as a small mock-Flemish castle with a copper ibis on the roof. It sits at the head of Mount Auburn Street, only a short distance from Harvard Square. *Courtesy of D. Peter Lund*

The Ibis vs. Communishm

Unfortunately, for the University of Moscow, Updike and the *Lampoon* wanted their Ibis back. Desperate to retrieve it, *Lampoon* staff members are said to have sent a telegram to Senator Joseph McCarthy suggesting that their rival's prank was more Red than Crimson and demanding an investigation.

According to the April 22, 1953, *Crimson*, Harvard and Radcliffe students rose in protest against the *Lampoon*'s attempt to take the Ibis away from the Russian people. Over three hundred Radcliffe students endorsed a petition demanding, "That the Ibis be left with the Russians, to whom it now belongs by right of courtesy."

The *Lampoon* was not amused. Updike stated, "The *Crimson* pranksters seem to have forgotten the rights of property. It's deplorable that they've carried college jokes into the arena of international relations."

In the April 22, 1953, *Crimson*, Maccoby and Abrams responded, "We are sorry that the supposed funny men of the *Lampoon* do not realize that humor is a great panacea for the world's ills and a strategic weapon in the present fight against Communism. It is sad, indeed, that such a petty sense of property has caused the *Lampoon* to crawl sniveling and whining to the State Department. It is a move that can only sour the nation's laughter. For the State Department to take a hand in returning the bird would be nothing short of appeasement."

The *Lampoon,* however, got its Ibis back after its treasurer spoke to the USSR representatives in their New York headquarters.

Epilogue

Almost fifty years later, the *Lampoon* retaliated. In 2000, *Lampoon* staffers liberated the *Crimson's* president's chair and gave it to the Prime Minister of Iceland as a symbol of peace and non-aggression between the United States and the nation of Iceland (*Crimson*, January 26, 2000). The president's chair is now chained to a wall in the Crimson building.

Ancient Egyptians considered the Ibis to be sacred.
Courtesy of D. Peter Lund

13

Chapter Thirteen:

MIT and Hackers

Gentlemen, you are about to play football for Yale against Harvard. Never in your life will you do anything as important.

T.A.D. Jones, Yale football coach, circa 1920

Two days before the bombardment of Ft. Sumter in 1861, the Commonwealth of Massachusetts approved a charter for the incorporation of the "Massachusetts Institute of Technology and Boston Society of Natural History." The institute's first students were admitted in 1865, only four years later. William Barton Rogers, a natural scientist, is credited with having the vision to establish MIT, a precedent-setting educational institution intended to meet the technical challenges of the United States as it became increasingly industrialized. Rogers believed that an education, which combined teaching with research, would produce the men needed to lead the country's economy.

By 1897, the Institute was the nation's largest and most complete school of applied science and engineering. Employing over fifty faculty and enrolling a thousand students, it offered curriculums in architecture (1865), electrical engineering (1882), sanitary engineering (1889), naval architecture and marine engineering (1895), aeronautical engineering (1914), meteorology (1928), nuclear physics (1935), and artificial intelligence (1960s). Until the campus moved across the Charles River to Cambridge in 1916, MIT was known as "Boston Tech."

MIT has a world-famous reputation for its brilliant students, who excel in everything from science and engineering to hacking. Pranks — known as hacks in MIT terms — are a long-hallowed MIT tradition. The earliest documented prank occurred in the nineteenth century when a mild contact explosive was sprinkled on the drill room floor to add a big bang to the assembly. Since MIT is a top engineering school, many of the hacks have a strong scientific component, but columns have been turned into candy canes at Christmas, university presidents' offices have disappeared, and 199 seats bolted to the floor in a lecture hall have been reversed so that they faced the back of the room. Almost all of these hacks amuse and entertain.

MCMXVI
MASSACHVSETTS INSTITVTE OF TECHNOLOG

One of the most famous hacks or pranks was the Blob, which along with two associated hacks, occurred during the 1982 Harvard-Yale game.

Before the game, MIT hackers smuggled into the Harvard stadium a black weather balloon, a hydraulic ram powered by Freon gas to lift the balloon out of the ground, and a vacuum-cleaner motor to inflate it. They planted all of this under the 45-yard line. Between 1 and 5 a.m., the perpetrators traveled back and forth to Harvard, locating an unused 110-volt circuit in the stadium and running buried wires from the stadium circuit to the burial site for the device. The hackers used manual control in order to time the detonation so as not to disrupt the game.

Tension was high during the game. Although Harvard had not scored against Yale since 1979, it was two touchdowns ahead with seven minutes and forty-five seconds remaining in the second quarter. According to the November 22, 1982, *Crimson,* "a huge black weather balloon swelled out of the ground at the 45-yard line. As coaches, players and 40,000 fans watched in amazement, the balloon, bearing the letters MIT inflated to almost six feet and exploded in a puff of smoke." With great consideration, the MIT students had set the Blob off between plays, so the outcome of the game wasn't unduly affected. Moreover, they thoughtfully attached a note to the balloon explaining that the device was not dangerous and contained no explosives.

MIT's Delta Kappa Epsilon fraternity took credit for the Blob. Harvard president Derek Bok commented: "A stunning practical joke — I give them full credit." President Paul E. Gray of MIT said: "There is absolutely no truth to the rumor that I had anything to do with it, but I wish there were."

The mission of MIT is to advance knowledge and educate students in science, technology, and other areas of scholarship that will best serve the nation and the world in the twenty-first century. *Courtesy of D. Peter Lund*

The Blob was only the first in a series of MIT pranks, which added a comic sideshow to the traditional rivalry of the Harvard-Yale game.

At halftime, during the same game, about forty MIT students, wearing the white pants and sweatshirts of the Yale Marching Band members, paraded onto the field. They lay down, and used their bodies to spell out MIT!

The third prank came about ten minutes into the fourth quarter, when MIT students distributed red and white placards to Harvard fans. The unsuspecting fans were told the cards spelled "Beat Yale." On cue, the thirteen hundred spectators raised their cards, spelling out MIT.

Interestingly, three independent hacking groups dreamed up these three hacks. It was a coincidence that they all targeted the same Harvard-Yale game.

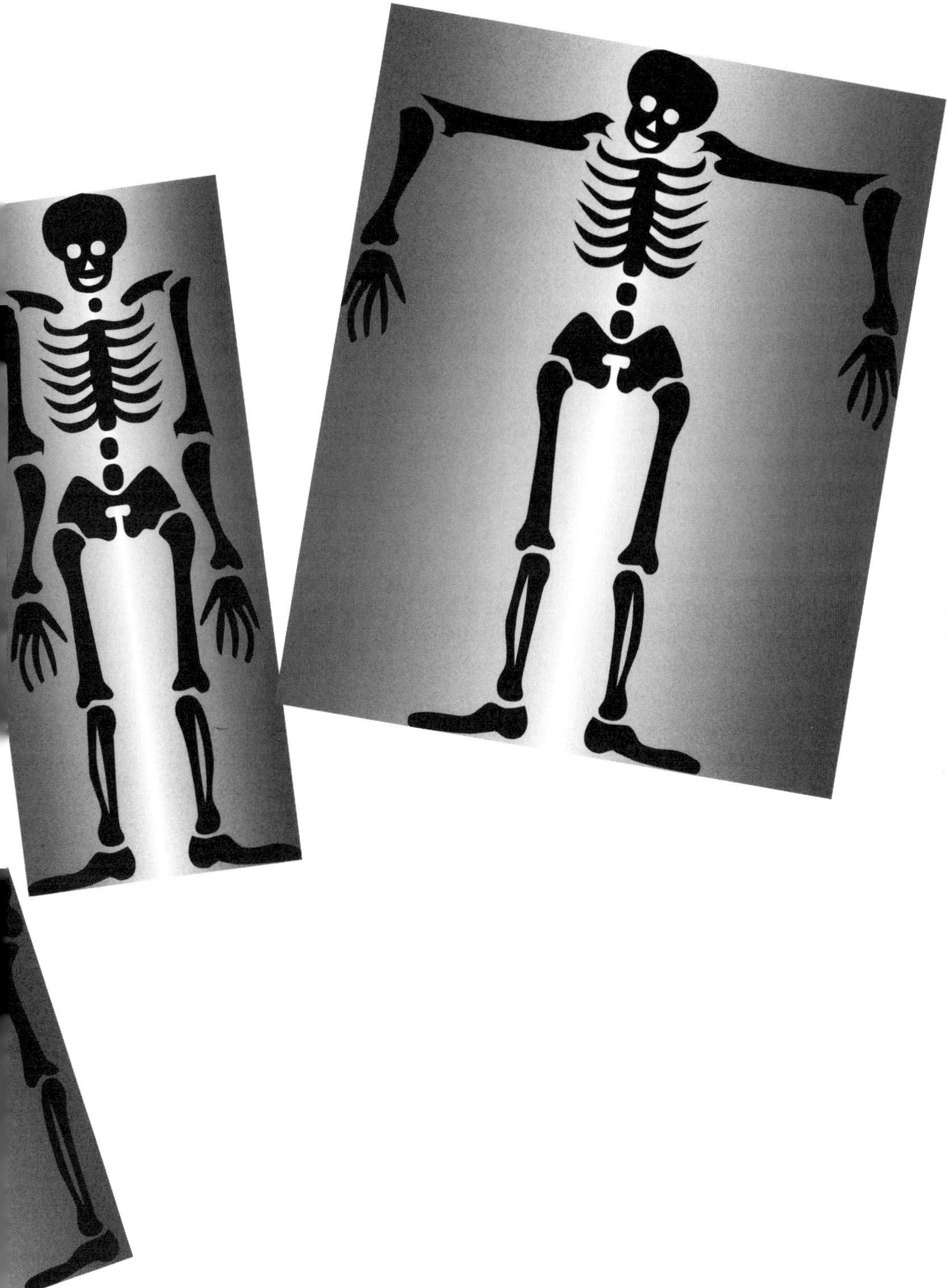

14

Chapter Fourteen:

The Smoot

Completed in 1891, the Harvard Bridge (also known locally as the "MIT Bridge" or the "Massachusetts Avenue Bridge") carries Massachusetts Avenue (Route 2A) from Back Bay, Boston, to the Cambridge flats, the ultimate site of MIT. The longest bridge over the Charles River, it's also the oldest. The MIT campus is on the Cambridge side, but many of the university's fraternities are in Boston.

During Massachusetts winters, the walk across this bridge can seem to take forever as you are buffeted by the wind and snow. In the fall of 1958, the pledge masters at MIT's Lambda Chi Alpha house challenged the pledges to mark the bridge so that a student crossing the bridge would know how far it was to the other side without looking up — and getting his eyes full of snow. The pledge masters decided that the unit of measurement would be the length of Oliver Reed Smoot, Jr., the shortest member of the pledge class. Mr. Smoot may have protested, but he is commemorated in the Halls of Measurement even today.

On a night in October, the pledges responded to this test of their abilities and to Mr. Smoot's fortitude. They laid Mr. Smoot, end over end, painting a white mark at every 5-foot and seven-inch interval. Given that Mr. Smoot is 5'7" tall (or 170 cm), measuring the bridge from the zero Smoot mark yields a bridge length of 364.4 Smoots and one ear long, or about 619 meters. Other sources give the length of the bridge as approximately 660 meters.

Being good engineers, MIT students knew the importance of regular maintenance. As the years passed, the fraternity members regularly painted length markers at 10-Smoot intervals to remind pedestrians that the bridge is 364.4 Smoots and one ear long. Eventually, the Boston police came to use these marks, to indicate the location where traffic accidents occurred on the bridge. Even today, you can see the markings indicating how many Smoots you have traveled.

The Harvard Bridge (also known locally as the "MIT Bridge" or the "Massachusetts Avenue Bridge") is the longest and the oldest bridge over the Charles River. *Courtesy of D. Peter Lund*

The agency responsible for the bridge, the Metropolitan District Commission, decided to preserve the original Smoots as part of the legend of the bridge. *Courtesy of D. Peter Lund*

The Smoot received some official recognition years later when the bridge's walkways required resurfacing. Some thought that it should be re-measured, and they could use the measurement device since Stephen Smoot, the son of Oliver Smoot, was an MIT junior. On the other hand, he was 5'11," which would distort the old calibrations. The agency responsible for the bridge, the Metropolitan District Commission, decided to preserve the original Smoots as part of the legend of the bridge.

After graduating from MIT, Mr. Oliver Smoot studied law and had a distinguished legal career. He became chairman of the board of the American National Standards Institute (ANSI) from 2001 to 2002 and President of the International Organization for Standardization (ISO) from 2003 to 2004. A fitting reward for the man who was the actual physical prototype of a Smoot.

15

Chapter Fifteen:

The Piano Drop

Engineers like to measure things. They like to whip out their calipers, their level plumbs and slide rules and measure what happens when. They also like to drop things. To brighten up a dull grey day in the winter, 1,600 pink and green ping-pong balls were dropped by remote control from the ninety-foot domed ceiling of MIT's Lobby 7. MIT students calculated that they fell at a rate of approximately ten per second, taking more than two and a half minutes for all the balls to drop.

One day, an MIT student named Bruno wondered how big the hole would be if an upright (not a grand but an upright) piano was tossed off the sixth floor onto the alley outside of Baker Hall. Now, Baker Hall had a worn out piano that needed to be discarded. The curious students and Bruno decided that a simple, easy, and even cheap experiment would be to toss the old piano from the top of the six-story Baker Hall and measure the cubic centimeter volume of the dent in the asphalt street. They even filmed and recorded this innovative experiment (aka "Musical Gravitational Demonstration") on October 24, 1972.

They discovered that the upright piano was moving at forty-three miles per hour at point of impact. The Bruno reading was 1,158 cubic centimeters. To be sure they got their figures correct, the students performed this experiment at least six more times, getting rid of many decrepit upright pianos. This drop technique was an effective way of not overloading the local landfill! Ultimately, the alley along Baker Hall was no longer obliterated by destroyed pianos but by new construction.

16

Chapter Sixteen:

The Great Dome

The 150-foot high great dome on top of the Barker Engineering Library defines MIT's campus. Internally, this space has served as a library reading room since 1916, when the Institute moved to Cambridge from Boston. Externally, this great dome is like a red flag to those creative MIT students. They have turned it purple for the start of the term, green to highlight its new environmentally friendly (green!) LED lighting system, and red, white, and blue to celebrate the Fourth of July. It has been transformed to a birthday cake for the University's centennial in 1961, a pumpkin for Halloween, and a giant beanie cap. A large screw, a piano, a massive Olympic gold medal, and snowmen have adorned it. By the beginning of the 1980s, dome decorating was an anticipated Halloween rite.

In 1979, one group of students, later known as the Burton One Outdoor Breast Society or (BOOBS), decided that the dome had a remarkable resemblance to the female breast. In order to augment this likeness, they constructed a giant pink nipple and aureole to scale. They had several problems placing it on top of the great dome. The nipple was spotted in the transport car; a cleaning woman caught them transporting it. During their fourth attempt, they were able to install a collapsible nipple. They named their work Mamma Maxima Scientiae.

In 1999, students converted the great dome into an oversized replica of the droid R2D2 from "Star Wars." The campus police discovered the red, white, blue, and black lightweight mesh fabric panels representing the robot's sensors and lights on the dome during routine patrol early in the morning.

At the top of the dome is a twenty-foot wide flat platform. Many objects have appeared on the dome, which is quite remarkable, given that the platform is accessible only through a small hatch. These objects range from a giant working propeller beanie to a piano. During 1979, inspired hackers placed a large fiberglass cow from the Hilltop Steak House on the platform. When the cow was returned, the Hilltop's management placed a mortarboard on her head and a diploma in her mouth.

In 2003, the campus celebrated the hundredth anniversary of the first controlled powered flight. A facsimile of the Wright Brothers' airplane was parked on the great dome. Inside the plane, a dummy figure of one of the brothers was along for the ride.

That same year a giant Mylar heart appeared on the great dome on Mother's Day. It was emblazoned with the word "MOM." It's rumored that one of the hackers was so busy for finals that he forgot to mail a Mother's Day card to his mom. When the errant son realized this, he decided to send his love so that everyone in the neighborhood of the dome knew that he remembered his mom on Valentine's Day.

On the morning of September 11, 2006, a 25-foot long fire truck on the great dome commemorated the five-year anniversary of the 9/11 attacks. Although MIT has no fire department, the side of the truck read "MIT FIRE DEPT." Inside the cab was a mock fireman. Two Dalmatian dogs pranced alongside the ladder, and a fire hose and pressure gauges were attached to the back of the truck. The rotating red light on top of the cab flashed at night.

One beautiful spring morning in May 1994, a white MIT campus police cruiser, complete with flashing lights, appeared on the top of the dome. A police officer with a gun and a box of

The MIT dome has been the focus of many, many pranks over the years. *Courtesy of D. Peter Lund*

donuts sat inside the car. A yellow diamond-shaped sign on the back window proclaimed, "I break for donuts." The car, numbered "pi," also sported a pair of fuzzy dice and an MIT Campus Police parking ticket ("no permit for this location").

The car turned out to be the metal outer shell of a Chevrolet Cavalier attached to a multi-piece wooden frame, carefully assembled on the roof over the course of one night. Not only did the local TV stations air footage of the car — some of which later wound up on national news — but the AP story spread to newspapers around the globe, from California to Korea and even Israel.

On Monday evening, a slide at the Lecture Series Committee movie read: "MISSING: one white and blue patrol car. If found, call x3-1212." The phone number was, of course, the number for the MIT Campus Police.

Students once placed an antique wooden phone booth stolen from outside the president's office on the great dome. They rigged it so both the lights and telephone worked. Campus police, puzzling about what to do about the booth, were astounded when the phone began to ring. They stared up at the ringing phone wondering what to do. Calling their supervisor, they asked him, "What should we do?"

Their supervisor replied, "Well...why don't you answer it?"

You need a sense of humor at MIT.

17

Chapter Seventeen:

The Legendary Inventors

Creative geniuses didn't just attend Cambridge universities learning how to conquer the inaccessible. They often stayed on to make possible the improbable in the high-growth, technology-focused businesses in Cambridge and the surrounding area. One fabled Cambridge-based company created hundreds of products and inventions in its laboratories since its 1886 beginnings.

Until its demise in 2002, Arthur D. Little, Inc. (ADL) was considered a premier research, development, and engineering consulting firm. Literally, hundreds of products and inventions for companies and government entities were developed in its laboratories. ADL has described itself as "the last place on earth where private enterprise really works" (Kahn, p. 12).

ADL focused on problem solving. In 1902, it was asked to resolve a problem for the New England Telephone and Telegraph Company. Its electrical contacts at the Milk Street station were malfunctioning, and nobody could figure out why. Company founder, Arthur Dehon Little eliminated all possible suspects until he found the culprit: the ash particles from a nearby restaurant's incinerator falling on its equipment.

Another staff member, Ernest Crocker, was able to recognize 9,000 distinct odors. At one point, Coca-Cola Company was debating whether it should engage ADL for a certain job. Crocker collected about a dozen bottles of Coke from different periods. He uncapped one after another, sniffed thoughtfully and announced the age of each correctly. ADL got the job! (Kahn, p. 76)

ADL worked on plastic body armor, powdered milk and eggs, a solution called Dog Drag, which when applied to shoes, could throw bloodhounds off the scent, and a noisemaker that simulated an artillery barrage, allowing infantry troops to advance fearlessly while the enemy cowered in fear. Among other things, it modernized the Saudi Arabia phone system, designed experiments for the Apollo space station, constructed an antitheft device for automobiles, and created a mattress turner.

Of Silk Purses & Lead Balloons

For years, the saying, "You can't make a silk purse of a sow's ear" has discouraged creativity and enterprise. Dr. Little challenged his staff to create "silk" purses out of sows' ears. He not only wanted to demonstrate this possibility to skeptics of chemistry but to impress bankers who might want to invest in artificial substitutes for silk. At the completion of the project, Dr. Little stated, "We resolved...to prove that it was false, and we have done so. We have made a silk purse of a sow's ear."

The chemists found that the viscous liquid emitted from ducts in the silkworm's head turned to silk after contact with air. Following this lead, the lab purchased one hundred pounds of authentic sows' ears, which they reduced to ten pounds of glue and then into gelatin. After much experimentation, the chemists produced fine "silk" strands, which were dried, dyed, and woven into a silky material. They then made two ten-inch long "silk" purses.

The company freely acknowledged that the two "silk" purses, expensive to produce, had more value as conversation starters than as items intended for practical use. The firm exhibited them at trade shows and promotional events. "We frankly admit," the company stated, "that it is not very strong or very good silk, and that there is no present industrial value in making it from glue."

The report about the project concluded: "Things that everybody thinks he knows only because he has learned the words that say it are poisons to progress. The only way to get ahead is to dig in, to study, to find out, to reason out theories, to test them." ADL presented one of the purses to the Smithsonian's National Museum of American History and displayed the other in its boardroom. (Contributed by Irving J. Arons, Product Technology 1969-1994.)

The Lead Balloon Contest

In March 1977, Jim Birkett, an ADL senior staff member suggested the firm sponsor a contest to see if any of its staff members could create a lead balloon that could fly. Thus began The Great Lead Balloon Contest.

On May 16, 1977 in the Acorn Park courtyard, three balloons were prepared for takeoff. One burst at the seams while being inflated. Another made it twelve feet off the ground. The third snapped its tether and headed toward Logan airport — about six miles from ADL. Somewhat later, a startled Delta Airlines pilot spotted it heading eastward toward Europe at 4,000 feet.

The event was covered by several local newspapers, as well as a local Boston TV station. Once again, the scientists at Arthur D. Little had done the impossible and shown that lead balloons could be made to fly.

18

Chapter Eighteen:

The Tell-Tale Bite

By mid century, the face of Boston was changing radically. The hills on the Shawmut peninsula were leveled, and the mud flats filled. The land reclamation of Back Bay began, and the old water line disappeared. Land values increased dramatically, making these ventures profitable. The remaining traces of the original city are in the names (Mount Vernon Street) and in the narrow crooked North End streets, which have kept their original circuitous routes that allowed them to avoid the hills.

From 1844 to 1854, Boston led the nation in foreign trade. The great merchant fleets still operated under sail, but the demand for speed brought in the clipper ship. Boston ships dispatched hopeful gold miners and goods to San Francisco, and those in the shipping industry garnered great profits.

A well-known figure in the streets of Boston was sixty-year-old Dr. George Parkman. He walked daily, wore a top hat, and had a protruding chin. Some even called him "Old Chin." A graduate of Harvard College and Harvard Medical College in 1813, Dr. Parkman was interested in remedying the terrible state of asylums for the mentally ill. Much to his disappointment, he was not appointed director of the new Asylum for the Insane (ultimately McLean Hospital). Subsequently, he concentrated on his business interests.

Dr. Parkman came from a very good family. His father owned most of Boston's West End and two towns that were named after him: Parkman, Maine and Parkman, Ohio. He had two wives and eleven children, all of whom had married well. Before he died in 1835, he appointed his son, George, who was already known for his miserly ways, to manage his estate. Seeing a good way to make his fortune, our Dr. Parkman bought more Boston real estate, from the North End to South Cove to the West End, including many dilapidated tenements. Everyone knew him—that bent figure with the chin jutting forward would walk the city each day to collect his rents, to get interest paid on his loans, and to keep an eye on things. He never used a horse for transportation; some say because he didn't want to spend the money. A good Bostonian, he knew that money didn't grow on trees, that a penny saved was a penny earned, and that a fool and his money were soon parted. People said he knew how to squeeze a nickel till the buffalo screamed.

An astute businessman, he sold the land for the new Harvard Medical School and the Charles Street jail. They say Dr. Parkman was worth approximately half a million dollars in 1849.

Now, Dr. Parkman was a privileged man. He lived the life of a gentleman surrounded by his family and friends. Perhaps his inherited wealth helped him afford it. Not everyone is so fortunate. They may want to keep up with their social milieu, but they can't afford the cost.

Dr. John White Webster, a professor of chemistry and geology, was a man who lived beyond his means. A Boston blueblood, he too had venerable connections in the Boston area. He also graduated from Harvard College and Harvard Medical School, practiced medicine in the Azores, where he published his first book, and married Harriet Hickling, the mother of his four daughters.

Once Professor Webster returned to Boston, he entered private medical practice. Being singularly unsuccessful, he changed careers and was appointed a lecturer of chemistry, mineralogy, and geology at Harvard Medical College. Although he was an affable man, his students considered him a dull teacher. Living paycheck to paycheck, he sold his house and rented another on Garden Street, Cambridge. Having grown up in the Azores, Harriet wanted her daughters to live better than she had. "Please, John," she would beg, "the girls need new wardrobes, if they are going to perform at our next musical evening." Or "new shoes." Or "a trip to the country." A loving father, Professor Webster didn't know how to say no. Instead, he was forced to borrow money to keep up appearances and provide for his lovely daughters and wife.

Our story begins when, in 1842, Dr. Parkman lent $400 to Professor Webster. Now debt occurs as a result of actions taken over a period of time. The ending of debt can be happy if you get out of it or sad if you get further and further into it. Unfortunately, Professor Webster got deeper and deeper into a fiscal mess. He kept on borrowing from others. In 1847, Professor Webster gave Dr. Parkman a note for $2,432, which represented his unpaid balance and a further loan. To secure this, he mortgaged his personal property, including his mineral collection. In 1848, still in financial distress, he borrowed $1,200 from Robert Gould Shaw, Sr. making over to him the minerals that already stood as collateral for his loan to Dr. Parkman.

A prominent focal point, the 195-foot high Memorial Hall tower was erected in 1874. In 1878, copper ornamentation was added to the original slate tower; a bell and four clock faces were installed. *Courtesy of Siobhan Theriault*

When Shaw, Dr. Parkman's brother-in-law and partner, mentioned this new loan to him, Dr. Parkman drew himself up and stuck his chin out a bit further. "Wait," he said, "That security is not secure. It is already mortgaged to me."

"No, Webster said it was free and clear."

"It's not. It's mine."

"What do you want to do?"

"That man is a crook. I'm being cheated! And after all I've done for him!"

Enraged, Dr. Parkman began to hound Professor Webster at the Medical College, his lecture card parties, and concert suppers. Everywhere Professor Webster went, Dr. Parkman would appear with his accusatory looks and his protruding chin.

On November 22, 1849, Dr. Parkman went to Cambridge to look for Webster and asked the Harvard cashier to give him the money from the sale of Webster's lecture tickets to repay Webster's debt. He announced, "Webster is neither an upright nor honorable man."

When the cashier repeated this comment to Professor Webster, the latter knew he was in trouble. The two men had many of the same friends, and Dr. Parkman had a great deal of influence with many powerful people. He couldn't afford to have Dr. Parkman say bad things about him. Adding to his stress, Dr. Parkman wrote Professor Webster, threatening exposure and disgrace. Finally, to compound the problem, he walked into Professor Webster's office demanding, "I want my payment. This is outrageous."

The following Friday, Professor Webster decided to take the upper hand. He called early in the morning at Dr. Parkman's house to propose a meeting that afternoon. Between noon and 1 p.m., Dr. Parkman left his home dressed in his black frock coat, dark pantaloons, purple silk vest with dark figured black stock, and black hat. He was planning to go to the Harvard Medical College, where he had an appointment with Professor Webster.

Dr. Parkman was never seen again.

By Sunday of that weekend, everyone was talking about the disappearance of Dr. Parkman. Many meaningful exchanges behind gloved hands took place at church that morning. Professor Webster went to Boston, telling everyone how Dr. Parkman had come to see him in Cambridge that Friday and how he had paid Dr. Parkman what he owed him. He even visited Dr. Parkman's family, although they thought him more hasty than usual.

The Harvard Medical School janitor, Ephraim Littlefield, was responsible for cleaning the doctors' rooms and laboratories, starting their fires, and whatever else they asked. He was a questionable sort, having sold cadavers to students for dissection at $25 a body. He and his wife shared the lower floor of the College with Professor Webster's laboratory. He had known both men for years and despised Professor Webster. Several days after the murder, when Professor Webster met Littlefield on the street, he asked, "Did you see Dr. Parkman at the College the previous week?"

"Yes, I did. On Friday around 1:30 p.m."

Professor Webster banged his cane on the ground. "Did you see Dr. Parkman anywhere in the building after 1:30? Did he come to my lecture room?"

"No," replied Littlefield.

"Good. I paid off my debt to him you know, on that Friday."

Several days later, when Professor Webster arrived at the college early, Littlefield spied him moving from the furnace to the fuel closet and back, making eight separate trips. Later in the day, the furnace was burning so hard that the wall on the other side was hot to the touch. Littlefield found that most suspicious. Then Professor Webster gave him a turkey for the Thanksgiving holiday. "Can you imagine that," Littlefield said to his wife, "that man gave me a turkey."

"Maybe he wants something," commented his wife.

"Hmm. Maybe you're right. He has never given me anything before."

"Perhaps you're being bribed!"

The next day, the suspicious Littlefield discovered human bones in the Professor's quarters. He reported it to the police, who arrested Professor Webster. They also pulled more bones out of the furnace. When they investigated the privy, they found a mass of viscera.

On December 6, the family held a funeral for Dr. Parkman, whose grisly remains had been positively identified in the privy and furnace. Thousands of spectators lined the streets to watch the funeral procession. Some five thousand had even taken a tour of the medical college to see where the grisly deed had occurred.

After Webster's arrest, Bostonians were reluctant to believe that one of their own had killed and dismembered another. Longfellow's wife wrote:

Boston is at this moment in sad suspense about the fate of poor Dr. Parkman... You will see by the papers what dark horror overshadows us like an eclipse. Of course we cannot believe Professor Webster guilty, bad as the evidence looks.... Many suspect the janitor, who is known to be a bad man and to have wished for the reward offered for Dr. Parkman's body. He could make things appear against the doctor, having bodies under his control. I trust our minds will be soon relieved, but, meanwhile, they are soiled by new details continually. I went to see poor Mrs. Webster on Saturday, the day after her husband's arrest, but of course was not admitted. What a terrible blight upon her life and that of the girls!

††††††††††

On March 19, 1850, with Chief Justice Lemuel Shaw of the Massachusetts Supreme Judicial Court presiding, the trial began. Accounts say that 60,000 people witnessed at least part of the twelve-day trial; bailiffs rotated people in and out of the courtroom every ten minutes. Journalists came from as far as London, Paris, and Berlin. The country — even the world — was fascinated.

This precedent-setting case altered the entire process of investigating death in the United States, changing legal trials in the United States forever. The prosecutors lacked primary evidence because Dr. Parkman's body was missing. Instead, they used expert witnesses who told the jury that the forensic evidence introduced at trial (bones, bone fragments, and related items) belonged to Dr. Parkman. Although this is common procedure today, it wasn't in 1850. The judge even allowed prosecutors to introduce a skeleton so the jury could understand how the recovered parts fit into a normal human skeleton.

The dentist, who had made Parkman's false teeth, was the most significant witness. The authorities had found false teeth at the crime scene. The dentist recognized them as Dr. Parkman's because he had made them to fit Dr. Parkman's protruding jaw. It was the first time dental evidence had been presented in a trial.

The jury voted unanimously that the remains were Parkman's, that Webster had killed him, and that he had done so deliberately. On April 1, Judge Shaw directed: "That you, John W. Webster, be removed from this place, and detained in close custody in the prison of this county; and thence taken...to the place of execution, and there be hung by the neck until you are dead. And may God, of His infinite goodness, have mercy on your soul!"

In June, Professor Webster, in a desperate bid to save his neck, wrote a confession. He admitted to killing Dr. Parkman in self-defense when the latter had become belligerent over his loan. He said that it was an unpremeditated rage, an act of passion and provocation, not a malicious murder. But it was too late. He was hung on August 30, 1850.

After his execution, Dr. Parkman's widow raised funds to help Webster's wife and children.

19

Chapter Nineteen:

The First Meetinghouse

In the early colonial era, the community was responsible for governing the town and for providing financial support for the meetinghouse and the minister. In turn, the meetinghouse dominated the religious and social life of the town — except for those who were Anglicans. The meetinghouse was also used for town meetings and university ceremonies.

Cambridge citizens had great respect for their first rude log meeting house. A central passage divided the interior, which was furnished with benches. The pulpit for the preacher, who was a scholar, was a plain desk. The ruling elders sat below the pulpit and the deacons a little lower still, facing the congregation, where men sat on one side and women on the other side of the passage. The boys were seated in the gallery with a tithing man armed with a long pole to keep them in order.

In Cambridge, the congregation came on foot or horseback as early as 9 a.m. on Sunday morning and left about 2 p.m. in the afternoon. The church service consisted of prayer, singing, reading, and explaining the Scriptures in an hour-length sermon. An hourglass stood on the pulpit so the preacher could watch his time, but sometimes the preacher would turn this at the end of his hour. The congregation called this "taking another glass." Every Sabbath afternoon there was a collection, and people passed their offerings up to the deacons' seat. Sometimes they brought money; sometimes they brought food or products.

The first meetinghouse, a square rude building, was built near the corner of Dunster and Mount Auburn Streets in 1632. After its first minister, Thomas Hooker and his flock moved to Connecticut, Reverend Thomas Shepard, a Puritan leader, gathered a new church, the First Church, on February 1, 1636. In 1637, the General Court of Massachusetts met at the First Meetinghouse to banish Anne Hutchison from Massachusetts for "troubling the peace of the commonwealth and the churches there..."

In 1638, Reverend Shepard used his influence with the General Court of Massachusetts to build the College in Newtowne (later called Cambridge), where his evangelical preaching might benefit Harvard College students. Fortunately, the college faculty and students had a liberalizing influence on the more strict New England Puritans.

In 1648, a new church was erected near the present site of Dane Hall at Harvard Square. As there were no other places of worship in Cambridge for almost one hundred years, many prominent men, who were Anglicans, held pews in the meetinghouse. The Second Meetinghouse, 1652, and the third, 1706, and the fourth, 1756, stood in what is now the College Yard, in the corner now occupied by Lehman Hall.

In February 1774, the Provincial Congress met at the meetinghouse. The Massachusetts delegates met there in 1779 to frame the constitution of the Commonwealth, which the people ratified in 1780. Washington and his fellow soldiers worshipped there in 1775.

In 1717, Reverend Nathaniel Appleton became pastor and served for the next sixty years. His Doctor of Divinity degree was the second given by Harvard. General Washington often worshipped in his congregation. While Reverend Appleton was pastor, the delegates of the state's towns met in the meetinghouse to frame the state constitution. The First Provincial Congress presided over by John Hancock also met there. In 1825, Edward Everett welcomed General Lafayette there.

The Trinitarian-Unitarian controversy resulted in a permanent schism in 1829. Since the majority of the congregation favored Unitarianism, they retained ownership of the old building, but they decided to build a new meetinghouse. Designed by Isaiah Rogers and dedicated in 1833, the meetinghouse is now known as the First Parish Church. It has an early Gothic Revival feeling in its tall windows and pointed arches. Harvard College held its annual commencement ceremonies within the meetinghouse in the mid-eighteen hundreds. Harvard College Presidents — Everett, Sparks, Walker, Felton, Hill and Eliot — began their inaugural terms there as well. The parish house was built in 1902, and the interior of the meetinghouse remodeled in 1914. The Crothers chapel was dedicated in 1941.

20

Chapter Twenty:

Old Burying Ground

Go into Burying-Place, Children; you will there see Graves as short as your selves. Yea, you may be at Play one Hour; Dead, Dead the next.

-- Cotton Mather

††††††††††

Most seventeenth century New Englanders lived each day in preparation for judgment and death. Death was a reality for them, striking people of all ages, not just the old. One half or fifty-one of the 102 Pilgrams who landed at Plymouth in 1620 died during the first winter. One child in ten died during the first year of life. Most early New Englanders lived each day in preparation for death and judgment, and they educated their children to do the same. Ministers frightened congregations with graphic descriptions of Hell and the horrors of eternal damnation.

Between First Parish Church and Christ Church lies the Old Burying Ground, which was originally part of the seventeenth century common lands. It was fenced in 1635. Early gravestones were inscribed but had no design because the Puritans thought that the Second Commandment prohibited the use of graven images. The original headstones faced east, so that on the morning of the Day of Resurrection the bodies would look towards God.

By the eighteenth century, there was increasing desire to mark the grave and to make a memorial for the deceased. The skulls, which stemmed from the Puritan's fear of death, were replaced with cheerful cherubs. Late eighteenth century graves are marked with urns, swags, wreaths, or weeping willows.

No longer were children told to fear death; by the eighteenth century they were told that death permitted a reunion with God and their parents. In turn, adults were promised that a life of active piety assured salvation. Death was increasingly regarded as merely a temporary separation of loved ones.

WOUNDED
AT BUNKER HILL
DIED
IN THE ARMY HOSPITAL
LT. GOV. OLIVER'S

The peaceful Old Burying Ground in Cambridge goes back to 1635, about 130 years before Christ Church was built. It contains Stephen Day, first printer on this continent, Thomas Shepard, first pastor in Cambridge, William Brattle, Thomas Hilliard, and Reverend Nathaniel Appleton; and here, too, are Harvard presidents Dunster, Chauncey, Oakes, Leverett, Wadsworth, Holyoke, Willard, and Webber. A monument is dedicated to the memory of the three patriots (John Hicks, Moses Richardson, and William Marcy) who fell April 19 at Lexington.

Between First Parish Church and Christ Church lies the Old Burying Ground. *Courtesy of Siobhan Theriault*

*All houses wherein men
have lived and died
are haunted houses. --*
Longfellow

Bibliography

Daughters of the American Revolution. *A Historic Guide to Cambridge*. Cambridge, Massachusetts: 1907.

Bartoletti, Susan. *Black Potatoes.* Boston, Massachusetts: Houghton Mifflin Company, 2001.

Barczewski, Stephanie L. *Titanic: A Night Remembered*. London, England: Hambledon and London, 2004.

Coffey, Michael (ed). *Irish in America.* New York, New York: Hyperion, 1997.

Crawford, Mary Caroline. *The Romance of Old New England Rooftrees.* Boston, Massachusetts: L.C. Page & Company, 1903.

The Romance of Old New England Churches. Boston, Massachusetts: L.C. Page & Co., 1903.

Dana, Henry Wadsworth Longfellow. *The Craigie House: The Coming of Longfellow* (1837-1841). Cambridge, Massachusetts: 1939.

Dolan, Edward. *The Irish Potato Famine. New* York, New York: Benchmark Books, 2003.

Drake, Samuel Adams. *Historic Mansions and Highways around Boston.* Rutland, Vermont: Charles E. Tuttle Company, 1971.

Gardiner, John Hays. *Harvard*. New York, New York: Oxford University Press, 1914.

Garrett, Wendell. *Apthorp House 1760-1960.* Cambridge, Massachusetts: Adams House, Harvard University, 1960.

Kahn, E. J. *The Problem Solvers.* Boston, Massachusetts: Little, Brown and Company, 1986.

Keneally, Thomas. *The Great Shame.* New York, New York: Nan A. Talese, 1999.

Laxton, Edward. *The Famine Ships: The Irish Exodus To America.* New York, New York: H. Holt, 1997.

Leibowitz, Brian M. *The Journal of the Institute for Hacks, Tomfoolery & Pranks at MIT.* Cambridge, Massachusetts: The MIT Museum, 1990.

Martin, Mary and E. Ashley Rooney. *Cambridge, Massachusetts: Past and Present*. Atglen, Pennsylvania: Schiffer Books, Ltd., 2007.

Merrill, Estelle (Ed.). *Cambridge Sketches by Cambridge Authors.* Cambridge, Massachusetts: Cambridge Young Women's Christian Association, 1896.

Peterson, T. F. *Nightwork.* Cambridge, Massachusetts: MIT Press, 2003.
Shapiro, Laura. *Julia Child.* New York, New York: A Lipper/Viking Book, 2007.
Steinberg, Neil. *If At All Possible, Involve A Cow*. New York, New York: St. Martin's Press, 1992.
Widener, P.A.B. *Without Drums.* New York, New York: G. P. Putnam's Sons. 1940.
Wilkinson, Jack. *Sunset over Craigie House.* Lawrenceville, Virginia: Brunswick Publishing Company, 1985.
Woodham-Smith, Cecil. *The Great Hunger.* New York, New York: E.P. Dutton, 1962.
Worthen, Dennis. "Andrew Craigie." *Journal of the American Pharmaceutical Association*, Vol. 42, No. 5, September 2002.

Newspaper/Internet

Arons, Irv. http://adlittlechronicles.blogspot.com.
Berman, Cindy and Diane Cardwell. "Techie Antics." *Harvard Crimson.* November 22, 1982.
Callan, Richard L. "100 Years of Solitude: John Harvard Finishes His First Century." *Harvard Crimson.* April 28, 1984.
Central Intelligence Agency. "A Look Back ...Julia Child: Life before French Cuisine." December 13, 2007.
Halberstam, David. "The Widener Memorial Room." *Harvard Crimson.* April 07, 1953.
Encyclopedia Titanica. www.encyclopedia-titanica.org/biography.
Herz-Roiphe, Daniel. "The Truth About John Harvard." *Harvard Crimson.* December 18, 2006.
Luna, Jessica. "Harvard-Yale Pranks." *Harvard Crimson.* November 15, 2006.
"Moscow University Gets Sacret Ibis: Russian Deputy Takes Bird." *Harvard Crimson.* April 21, 1953.
PBS. *Murder at Harvard.* 999-2003. PBS Online/WGBH.
"Poonsters Demand Russians Return Ibis. Fail to See Humor of Ibis Sitting on Spire of Red University." *Harvard Crimson.* April 22, 1953.
Ramsland, Katherine. "All about George Parkman." www.crimelibrary.com/notorious_murders/classics/george_parkman
"Sacred Cod Laid to Lampoon." *New York Times*. April 28,1933.
Seward, Zachary. "Lampoon, Crimson Face Off in Intra-Collegiate Rivalry." *Harvard Crimson*. June 7, 2004.
"Widener Gutenberg Bible Near Best Outstanding Specimen In Harvard Scarce Volume Collection." *Harvard Crimson.* November 10, 1949.

Old Burying Ground. *Courtesy of Siobhan Theriault*

Index